BATAAN DEATH MARCH

BATAAN DEATH MARCH
A Soldier's Story

James Bollich

Foreword by Jesse Knowles

PELICAN PUBLISHING COMPANY
Gretna 2003

First Pelican edition, 2003

ISBN: 1-58980-167-9

Printed in the United States of America

Published by Pelican Publishing Company, Inc.
1000 Burmaster Street, Gretna, Louisiana 70053

To my brothers, Andrew and Stephen,
who lost their lives fighting in the
European theatre of operations,
and to all the brave soldiers who died in battle
and in prisoner of war camps during World War II.

Contents

Foreword

James Bollich and I followed almost identical paths prior to and during World War II. We both joined the U.S. Air Corps at Barksdale Field, Shreveport, Louisiana, and were both assigned to the 27th Bombardment Group. Both of us took part in the 1940 maneuvers, and we both went overseas on the same ship, arriving in the Philippine Islands eighteen days before the outbreak of hostilities.

After the war started we both served as infantry soldiers in defending the Philippines because our planes never arrived as intended. Both of us were captured when Bataan was surrendered to the Japanese by American General Edward P. King, Jr., and we both made the Death March out of the peninsula to the concentration camp established by the Japanese at Camp O'Donnell. From there we went on a Japanese work detail to rebuild a large bridge that had been destroyed during the fighting. When the detail was abandoned, we were sent back to the prison camp at Cabanatuan.

From Cabanatuan we both became part of a group of prisoners selected to be moved to Manchuria, where we remained until freed by the Russian army at the end of the war. In Manchuria, even though we were quartered in several barracks, we somehow wound up in the same one. We were even in the same section of the barracks. Remember that all of the above was coincidental and neither of us had anything to do with it. Even after the war, when we returned to civilian life, we both took jobs in the petroleum industry.

Fifty years after the war ended, Jim put his thoughts and

recollection of events down in writing so that his family and others would know the part he played in defending the Philippine Islands, and his battle to survive as a prisoner of war. I did my writing fifty years ago in prison camp. It was in the form of a poem, which tells of our struggles and aspirations at the time. Now I would like to submit it as an addition to Jim Bollich's book, *Bataan Death March: A Soldier's Story.*

Jesse Knowles
Louisiana State Senator

They

Strange things were done under the tropic sun
By the men in khaki twill.
Those tropic nights have seen some sights
That would make your heart stand still.
Those mountain trails could spin some tales
That no man would ever like;
But the worst of all was after the fall
When we started on that hike.

'twas the 7th of December in '41
When they hit Hawaii as the day begun.
'twas a Sunday morning and all was calm
When out of nowhere there came the bombs.
It didn't last long but the damage was done—
America was at war with the Rising Sun.

Now over in the Philippines we heard the news;
And it shook every man clean down to his shoes.
It seemed like a dream to begin;
But soon every soldier was a fighting man.
Each branch was ready to do its part:
Artillery, Infantry, Nichols and dark.

And then they came on that Monday noon,
They hit dark Field like a typhoon.
That Monday night the moon was clear;
They razed Nichols from front to rear.
As the days went by more bombers came;

And soon only a few P-40's remained.
Then the orders came and said retreat,
That no man would be seen on the city streets.
So across the bay we moved at night
Away from Manila and out of sight,
Deep into the jungles of Bataan
Where 15,000 were to make a stand.

Here we fought as a soldier should.
As the days went by we spilled our blood.
Tho' the rumors came and went by night
That convoy never came in sight.

April 7th was a fatal day
When the word went around that we couldn't stay,
That the front line was due to fall;
So the troops moved back one and all.

The very next day the surrender came.
Then we were men without a name!
You may think here's where the story ends,
But actually here's where it begins.
Tho' we fought and didn't see victory
The story of that March will go down in history.

We marched along in columns of four
Living and seeing the horrors of war,
And when a man fell along the way
A cold bayonet would make him pay
For those four months he fought on Bataan.
Then they'd kill him 'cause he couldn't stand.

The tropic sun would sweat us dry
For the pumps were few that we passed by.
But on we marched to a place unknown,
A place to rest and a place to call home.
Home not that you might know,
But home to man that suffered a blow.

Then to O'Donnell Camp en masse
Some never back through those gates to pass.
In Nipa huts we lived like beasts,
Bad rice and camotes were called a feast.

Our minds went back to days gone by
When our throats were never dry;
Of our wives, our mothers and friends,
Of our bygone days and our many sins.
And about four thousand passed away
And how many more no man can say,
For no tombstone marks the spot
Where thirty to fifty were buried in a lot,
Piled together as a rubbish heap—
The remains of men Who were forced to retreat.

Now I want to state, and my words are straight,
And I bet you think they're true,
That if you gotta die it's better to try
And take them with you, too.

It's they that took us that fatal day,
It's they that made us pay and pay.
It's they that counted us morn and night,
It's they that again we wanted to fight,
It's they that made us as we are,
But it's not they that'll win this war,
For the men in khaki will come someday
And take us back to the U.S.A.

Introduction

Every soldier, who lived through the battles to defend the Philippine Islands against the Japanese invasion; who felt the pain of hunger and exhaustion while fighting these battles; who reluctantly destroyed his arms when his commanding general surrendered; who made the tortuous march out of Bataan and survived three-and-one-half years of unbelievable treatment and conditions in prisoner of war camps has a different story to tell. Now, after all these years have passed, I have told mine so that my family and friends, and whoever else that may be interested, will have some idea of the part one soldier played in this catastrophic episode.

I, as well as the others, do not consider ourselves heroes, but rather survivors. Why some survived, and others did not, no one will ever know. Did I survive because of the canteen of water I found on the Bataan Death March? Was it the can of warm rice that I picked up in the mud at the water well, where we madly made a dash for a drink? Not all of us succeeded or returned. Was it the timely picking and eating of leaves to stop my dysentery shortly after confinement at Camp O'Donnell prison camp? I do not know.

I would like to thank my nephew, James G. Atteberry, my brother, Charles, and my wife, Celia, for persuading me to write my story, because without their prodding and support, it would probably never have been written.

BATAAN DEATH MARCH

★ 1 ★

Entering the Service

I joined the service on August 23, 1940, at Barksdale Field, Shreveport, Louisiana, and was assigned to the 16th Bomb Squadron, 27th Bomb Group. I joined because Paris had just fallen to the Germans, and I felt that we would soon be at war.

I was in college at the time and had just finished my third semester. All the talk around school was about war, and it was hard to keep my mind on books. I was attending Southwestern Louisiana Institute (S.L.I.) in Lafayette through a government program called the N.Y.A. (National Youth Administration). We received $30 a month and had to work a full eight hours every other day. Because of this it was hard to schedule classes and also hard to study properly.

From our $30 pay we had to put out $18 each month for room and board, which left $12 for other essentials such as books, paper, pencils, etc. Because going to college was so difficult under these conditions, it seemed that the Army could not be any worse. It also appeared we would all be in the Army eventually anyway.

There was an Army recruiting office in Lafayette, so I went to talk to the recruiting officer. I told him that I was interested in the Air Corps and would like to become a pilot. He told me that with four semesters of college a person did not need to take a qualifying exam to get in flight school, and since I already had three semesters, he suggested the following: join the service at Barksdale and get my last semester at Centenary College in Shreveport. At this time the Army was encouraging people to go to school at government expense. This seemed great and was exactly what I was looking for. I told him that I would go to Barksdale Field and look it over and talk to him later.

School at S.L.I, let out early for the summer semester of 1940 because of the tremendous flooding that occurred at the time. I remember that the water was knee-deep on the campus and all classes and final exams were cancelled. I tried getting home during the flood but got only as far as Crowley, and could go no farther. I got as far as the Crowley courthouse, where the water was already chest-high.

I remember going into a small grocery store on Main Street to see if I could buy something to eat. The water was belt-high in the store and bread, boxes and other things were floating around. I found the owner standing on the counter; he said, "Take what you want, it is all ruined anyway." As I remember I took a small pack of crackers.

I got to Crowley by catching a freight train in Lafayette. The train was going out and coming in with refugees from the flood. Going out, they did not want anyone on it, so I had to sneak on after it started. Coming back from Crowley was easier because they thought I was a refugee from the flood. I was soaking wet and surely did look like I needed evacuation.

I was put in a box car that had previously carried cement, and when the train started, and got up speed, cement dust got on everyone and everything.

The door of the car had been left open and the wind coming in was causing bedlam, but there was no way to close it. When we finally reached Lafayette, I looked like a cement statue. Cement had gotten on my wet clothes and hair and had hardened, and I was miserable.

I could hardly wait to get back to my dormitory, and when I did get back I was shocked with what I found. The school had already turned my room over to a refugee family (a woman with small children), because they assumed that I had left campus. The woman felt bad about it, but I said it was OK. Just let me get towel, soap and clean clothes, and I would be fine. I did not think that I would ever get the cement out of my hair. Even after scrubbing it over and over, it still felt like nails.

A day or two later I finally got home by way of Opelousas but had to swim the bayou to get home. Luckily the house on the farm was not flooded. Maybe now you see why I joined the service.

After the flood waters went down I went back to get my things at school and was horrified to see the destruction all around. In the countryside hundreds of cattle, horses, mules, pigs etc. that had drowned. After seeing this I was definitely ready for the Army.

A few days after returning home I decided to go up to Shreve-port with a friend of mine to see what Barksdale was all about. I remember hitchhiking to Kinder and catching a freight train to Alexandria and on to Monroe.

Anyway, we hitchhiked on to Shreveport and finally got to Barksdale. I don't remember how long this trip took but riding that freight train was like riding a turtle. Slow, slow, slow and stopping constantly to let off cars and take on cars and always afraid that the car that you were in would be left behind.

After seeing Barksdale Field I felt that the place looked fine, and I made up my mind that I would return. I went home and told my parents what I planned to do. My mother was horrified and strictly against it. At the time I needed my parents' consent to join because of my age; I was 19. My father agreed to sign and convinced my mother to sign also. I remember her saying that if anything happened to me, she did not want to be blamed for letting me go to the Army.

With my papers signed I returned to the recruiting office in Lafayette where they put me on a train with about five or six others, which took us to Shreveport. It was a freight train and we rode in the caboose. It was as slow as the one I caught out of Kinder earlier.

We boarded the train early in the day in Lafayette and did not reach Barksdale until about 2 o'clock next morning. We had no food or drinks during the entire trip. When the train stopped in Shreveport, Army trucks were waiting for us, and they took us to the barracks at the field. It felt wonderful to finally have a place to stretch out and sleep, and I forgot about being hungry.

Next morning I was sworn in with the rest of the recruits. I had a choice of joining a weather squadron or a bombardment squadron. Of course I choose the bombardment squadron. I did not join the Army to study the weather. I joined to fight-that is what I thought. I was, therefore, assigned to the 16th Bomb Squadron of the 27th Bomb Group. At the time this group had B18A bombers and were considered top of the line. I remember hearing that they cost 1 million dollars each.

Army clothes and equipment at this time were in short supply, and we were not provided with clothes, etc. for quite some time. We reported for duty in our civilian clothes and it was a sight to see people training to march in black-and-white shoes.

Our duty for the first four weeks was to learn how to march and drill. Each morning after breakfast we recruits were told to report to a drill sergeant at the parade grounds for training. I did this for a week and a half, even though I was supposed to do it for four weeks.

This is what happened: The parade ground was mass confusion. New recruits were coming in every day and did not know where to go. Even those that had been here before could not remember what group they were in or who their drill sergeant was.

One particular morning the officer of the day decided he would straighten out the confusion once and for all. He designated four areas on the parade ground for the trainees. One area was for people that were in their first week of training, another area for the two-week people and another for four- and three-week people.

By the time the officer mentioned the three- and four-week people I caught on to what was going on so, instead of going to the area for two-week people, I went with the four-week people even though I was still in civilian clothes.

Finally when the officer of the day said, "Everyone with four weeks training fall out and report to his respective squadrons for active duty," I realized that I may have made a mistake. So, instead of reporting for active duty, I just wandered around the base for another couple of weeks.

When the first sergeant would tell the recruits to report to the parade ground for drill, I would just sneak off to the PX or wander around. I had enough training to know how to march, and I still wonder why it was necessary because I never did march again in the service.

While I was avoiding training, I would go to the quartermaster building now and then to see if I could get my Army clothes. I finally did after about three weeks. When four weeks had passed I reported to our first sergeant for duty. He never did know what I had done.

The clothing that we had was still essentially World War I. We had leggings, campaign hats, etc. at this time.

We were allowed $150 for clothing, but what a lot of soldiers were doing was holding back on spending the full amount, the reason being that you could still buy out of the service if you did not like it. A private could buy out for $75; a corporal, $50; and a sergeant, $25.

I did not know for sure how the Army would work out so I had the quartermaster outfit me for $75 and still have a credit of $75.

With $75 worth of clothes I had plenty, more than I had ever had before because at home I lived in hand-me-downs.

When I reported for duty at the hangar, I was assigned to sweeping hangar floors and washing planes. It was dull, and I wondered if this is what it was like in the service. I had by now registered to attend Centenary College and was anxious to get my last semester in so that I could enter flight school.

Our stay (27th Bomb Group) at Shreveport was short-lived, and before I could attend one class at Centenary we were packed up and on our way to Savannah, Georgia to open up a new field.

We went by train. At Savannah we lived in tents, and

things were rough compared to barracks living. Exams were given to find out who wanted to go to school and who was qualified. I took and passed the exams and shortly thereafter was on my way to aviation school at Love Field, Dallas.

The school in Dallas was great. It had just opened for Army schooling and I was in the second class of a group of twenty-five. Accommodations were excellent and the food was good, much better than what we were getting from our field kitchen in Savannah.

The school lasted about nine months, and I came out knowing everything there was to know about an airplane, but I still wanted to fly. When the school was over for my class, I was offered a position as instructor of drafting, but I turned it down. I wanted to get back with my outfit.

The class that I was in had a basketball team, and I was one of the players. There were only six of us, five players and one spare. I was mostly the spare because I had never played the game before. We played local teams in Dallas and turned out to be very good.

One of the guys on the team was from Sunset, Louisiana so he scheduled a game with his high school team, the game to be played in Sunset. The problem now was to get to Sunset and back in a weekend. For $15 we hired someone with a car to drive us down. We played the game, but I don't remember who won. Anyway I got to go home for a short while, and I remember my brother Andrew taking me back in town where I was to meet the car and guys going back to Dallas. This was the last time that I saw my brother.

When I got back to Savannah, I found my outfit packing up to go on maneuvers in Louisiana. Within a few days we were on our way by Army truck. At night we would stop, set up our mess tent, eat and hit the sack. We slept on the ground under a pup tent. It took us two or three days to reach our final stop, which was the airfield at Lake Charles. Here we lived in tents, again just as our first days in Savannah.

As far as I was concerned at the time, maneuvers were a

joke. Instead of having actual machine guns, anti-aircraft guns, foxholes, etc., there were wooden signs all around to indicate these. If the air raid siren went off we were supposed to run to one of these signs. The one way that maneuvers did apparently help us with down the line was to adapt us to hard, rough outdoor living. We were also on reduced rations which helped to prepare us for what was to come later on.

If an air raid occurred at night all lights were turned off (blackout) and everyone took off, going either to bed or to town. I mentioned earlier that when I joined the 27th Bomb Group, we had B18A's as our planes. At Savannah we changed to A-20A's, which was a fast-attack plane, but on maneuvers we changed again to dive bombers. Up to this time dive bombers were strictly a naval operation and now we were the first air-corp unit to train with them.

We would fly over the "enemy" and drop small sacks of flour on them. Referees would tell if we hit or missed, and the sides were scored accordingly. I don't remember how long the maneuver exercises lasted, but it seems that it was at least a month.

I remember it rained a lot and the area where our tents were was at times a sea of mud. The only real excitement that I can remember happening during maneuvers was when one of our pilots landed on the runway with his wheels still up. It really messed up the plane, but the pilot was not hurt. Another pilot overshot the field and went through a fence, over a road, and stopped in an adjacent field. No pilot damage, but another beat-up airplane.

We finally got word to pack up and head back home to Savannah. We had already gotten the word that as soon as we reached Savannah, we would need to pack again. This time to go overseas, but no one knew where as yet.

The trip back was uneventful. Again it was by truck and was a duplicate of the trip down.

When we reached Savannah we found that most of our gear that we left behind was already crated and ready to go.

As I recall, in about a week or so we boarded a train for San Francisco. All of our crates were stenciled with the letters PLUM, but no one knew what it meant. I should mention here that before we left Savannah, I was called to the first sergeant's office and told that

I did not have to go overseas if I did not want to. Of course I immediately rejected the idea and said I definitely wanted to go. To this day I don't know why this came up, because in talking to others in my outfit no one else had that opportunity. Since I had applied for flight school, it may be that I could have gone there.

I still don't know what PLUM stood for, but looking back now, apparently the P stood for Philippines, the L for the island of Luzon, but the U and M I do not know.

It took several days to cross the States, because we had to give way to every other train on the track. We always stopped at some God-forsaken spot far from any city or town with one exception, Laramie, Wyoming. Little did I know that one day I would be attending the university there. We stopped in Laramie at about

Two o'clock in the morning, and were told we could leave the train for a short while. Laramie was so small that there was no danger of anyone getting lost or in trouble.

I remember there were only one or two places open, and I believe they had prior notice of our arrival, otherwise the whole place would have been completely black. We complained when all we got for change was silver coins. I remember getting several silver dollars in change and hated it. Wish I had them now.

We finally left Laramie after the engines were again loaded with coal, and water was taken on. These coal engines made the cars on the train extremely dirty. We had regular sleepers on the train, and in the morning when a person woke up his sheets would be black with soot. Your nose would also be clogged up as well. Our clothes were filthy, because there was no way to bathe or change regularly. We had only what we could carry in our ditty bag.

Our next stop was at Salt Lake City. We were told we would be allowed off the train for a few hours so I thought I would try to locate my brother, Stephen, who was stationed nearby.

With a friend of mine we hired a taxi and took off for the base. From the gate, through the help of the guards, I was able to locate the barracks where he stayed, and there we found him sitting on his bunk. Needless to say he was surprised to see me, and I was very glad to see him.

He apparently had not heard that I was going overseas. Since we only had a short time to get back to the train, he said he would take us. With a borrowed car he drove us back by way of downtown back to the train. I told him goodbye, and that was the last time that I saw him.

One of the highlights of the trip was going through the mountains; they were spectacular. A scene I shall always remember is following the Feather River Valley out of the mountains. It was snowing heavily, and the ground was covered as well as the towering trees. Everything on the outside seemed so clean and fresh. You could even smell the evergreen forest over the odor of the coal smoke from our engines.

We kept losing altitude as we approached Sacramento, California and from there on into San Francisco. The train stopped at the docks, and all we had time to do was secure our footlockers from the car with our luggage and catch the boat to Angel Island. My luggage arrived in good shape, but others were not so fortunate. One of the boxcars with luggage broke loose from the train and was completely submerged in the bay. When it was finally retrieved everything in it was completely soaked.

The boat trip to Angel Island was very cold, because we were now in the fall of the year. I remember we stopped at Alcatraz Island to unload supplies. Alcatraz was still a Federal prison at the time. Once on Angel Island we were put in barracks and had no duty to perform.

I understand that some of the troops did have to help

with KP, but luckily I did not have to. The next few days were spent getting inoculations in preparation for going overseas. We went through in a line getting shots in both arms at the same time. Several of the guys passed out, but they got their shots anyway, even though they were out.

Early one morning we got word to pack our gear and get ready to board ship. I remember it was cold and foggy and dark when we boarded ferries that took us to the docks at San Francisco, where we then boarded the S.S. *Coolidge.*

Shortly after sunrise we pulled away from the dock and before long we were going under the Golden Gate Bridge. All we could see was the bottom of the bridge, because the upper part was completely hidden by fog. By the time we reached the bridge, several soldiers were already sea sick even though the bay was relatively calm.

The S.S. *Coolidge* was a lovely ship that normally carried civilian passengers to the Orient, but now it was being used to transport troops. We did not have state rooms, but slept in quarters comparable to regular Army transports.

We ate in the beautiful dining room, but not on china, but used our tin trays and mess kits. The food was typical army, not exceptionally good but adequate.

About the third day out we found out where we were going. Up to this time no one knew. Our squadron commander called us all together and told us that we were headed for the Philippine Islands. He told us that we were the first part of an expeditionary force being sent out to beef up the defenses of the Philippines. He said that it appears that we would soon be going to war with Russia. He probably said Japan, but back then I was sure he said Russia.

After this talk, I don't remember anyone getting very excited about it. We all went back to killing time and doing the things that we were doing before. Some people read, some gambled and some exercised. There was boxing going on, so I decided I would participate. I boxed as a Light-heavyweight at 165 pounds.

The first match that I had was with a corporal from my

outfit. When I saw who it was, I figured it would only be a sparring match between us and nothing real serious. How wrong I was, however, because he lit into me like he was going to tear me apart. When I realized that he was serious, I hauled back and knocked him out with a single blow. Winners got $3; losers got nothing.

After about a week at sea we arrived in Honolulu. We had about 8 hours shore leave so I did get to see some of the island. While I was there, I bought a very fine 35 mm camera with hopes of taking many pictures while I was overseas. Although I took many pictures, the only one that I ever saw was the last one taken. This I write about later.

Honolulu is the place where I finally learned the port and starboard sides of a ship. On large ships I still get lost and confused. I had to go out on deck and see which way the boat was traveling to locate myself.

We finally left the dock and as we pulled out of Pearl Harbor saw the ship with our planes just coming in. We never saw our planes again and little did we realize what would happen to Pearl Harbor in just a few short weeks.

Our next stop was Guam. Apparently Guam did not have a harbor and dock capable of handling our large ship, because we stayed well offshore. Supposedly we were delivering supplies to the island and taking on fresh water. We anchored offshore for five or six hours, and I recall some of the crew fishing for sharks. They had rope for a line and their hook was baited with a chicken. I don't think that they caught anything. It was shortly after they started fishing that we pulled anchor and headed once again for the Philippines. Guam was our last stop.

One or two days out of Guam we were approached by a Japanese war ship. It was probably a cruiser of some sort. It apparently looked us over and then took off. A few weeks later we would not have been so lucky. I still wonder if that Jap ship knew that they would soon be at war with us. They probably did.

I don't remember how long it took us to get to the

Philippines from Guam, but I am sure it was several weeks. It was the same old story on board ship: eat, sleep and try to find something to pass the time. One incident that occurred was really hilarious. You would have to know our squadron commander to appreciate this. He was a West Point graduate, and it showed. He walked around like a Caesar who demanded respect.

Anyway, we were below deck somewhere and this friend of mine (a large guy over 6 feet tall) saw this soldier dressed in khaki looking out of a porthole. The light where we were was not very good and it was hard to recognize anyone.

Anyway, my friend thought that he knew the soldier at the porthole so he grabbed him by the collar and seat of the pants and acted like he was going to throw him overboard. When the two recognized each other, I don't know who was the more surprised. My friend tried to offer some lame excuse, but our commander walked off without a word. I nearly died laughing. Unfortunately, my friend did not survive the war to laugh about it today. He died at Camp O'Donnell about a week or two after the surrender.

★ 2 ★

The Philippine Islands

One morning when I got up and went out on deck, I noticed islands all around us. We were finally in the Philippines. The islands looked so tropical with their lush growth and many palm trees. You could see the small bamboo huts on shore with their thatched roofs. People were seen on the beautiful sand beaches around their small boats, which were pulled up on shore. It was a beautiful sight after seeing nothing but water for many weeks. This looked like a place that I knew I would like.

Before long we were passing the Island of Corregidor going into Manila Bay. To our left was the Bataan Peninsula. We gave each a good hard look because this was the closest we had come to land since leaving the Hawaiian Islands. Little did we realize that in a few short weeks these two places would be our salvation, at least for a while. Across the bay, at a distance, the city of Manila could barely be seen. About this time we were told to assemble our gear and get ready for docking and debarking. This time I knew where port side was.

Just as soon as we got off the ship we were loaded into Army trucks and taken to Fort McKinley. The fort was located on the outskirts of Manila and was the home of the Filipino scouts. The scouts were trained and commanded by American officers and were not directly part of the Philippine Army. They were well trained and fought with distinction during our time of resistance which could not be said for the regular Philippine Army.

The barracks at Fort McKinley were two-story wooden

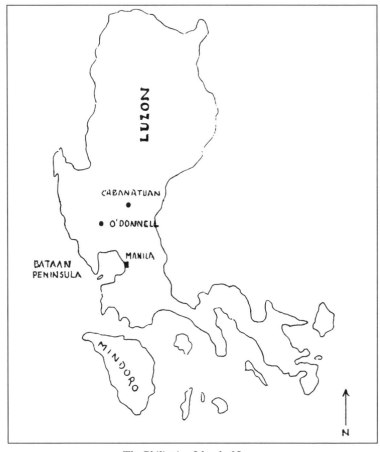

The Philippine Island of Luzon

buildings that were surrounded by a porch or veranda. Large trees kept them shaded. They looked very cool and comfortable compared to where we were. Our location was on the fort's drill field, where we had pitched our tents in the hot, tropical sun. There was no shade to be had and the tents were unbearably hot during the day and just as hot at night when the sun went down.

I should point out here that during peace time in the Philippines (prior to our arrival) the military was on duty only in the morning from eight o'clock to eleven o'clock. It was thought that a white person could not survive in the tropical sun after eleven o'clock. What a deal they had and, to top it off, time spent in the tropics (Hawaii included) counted as time-and-a-half toward retirement.

Another reason that we were so hot when we first arrived in the tropics was the fact that we still had on our winter uniforms. You recall we left the States in the fall, and it was bitterly cold when we left Angel Island. We finally traded in our winter gear for summer wear, but it was still hot. This is where I was first issued my pith helmet, and to this day it is still my favorite hat.

Tropical uniforms issued at Fort McKinley

The day after we arrived at Fort McKinley, we were read a message from General McArthur, who welcomed us to the island. This sounded nice and friendly, but the ending made you wonder about its sincerity. The message ended by saying that if we ever got in trouble with any Filipino, the army would consider the Filipino to be innocent and the American to be guilty. I did not expect to get into trouble, but this so-called welcome did not set too well with me and presumably a lot of others as well. It gave us the impression that McArthur cared more for the Filipinos than he did Americans. He had been in the islands so long that this was apparently true.

Living in tents was easier here than in the States, even considering the heat. The reason being that there was so much local help to rely on. There were Filipinos all over our camp site looking for something to do to make a little money. They would make up your cot, straighten up your tent, wash your clothes, shine your shoes, run errands for you, etc. You did not have to lift a finger around camp if you took on one of these guys. They even did all of the KP work for the outfit. All of this required very little money on our part, which was fortunate because we had very little to spend.

As long as I was at Fort McKinley (about two weeks) the only thing that I ever did was dig trenches around the fort. These were not foxholes, but long zig-zag trenches. We were undoubtedly preparing for war. This work was also difficult because a lot of it was in solid rock. I am sure that these trenches were never used, at least by our forces.

I only got to go into Manila one time and that was when the Japs attacked Hawaii. It was still night in the Philippines, but early in the morning in Hawaii when the Japs hit Pearl Harbor. There were four of us that went into town, and I recall that we went into a restaurant to eat and had trouble communicating with our waiter. We all ordered and this friend of mine decided to change his order at the last minute. He thought that he had conveyed his wishes to the waiter but lo and behold here came two orders instead of the changed one. We all laughed and the waiter laughed too, he not knowing what we were laughing about. We were all hungry enough to eat the extra dish and gladly shared in the cost.

From the restaurant we went on to see a movie. The movie was about Sergeant York, the American soldier who captured a bunch of Germans during World War I.

After the movie we took a tram or trolley back to the gate at Fort McKinley. Before going to our tent we decided to stop at our mess tent for something to drink before retiring and that is when we heard that Pearl Harbor was being bombed by the Japanese.

This message came from a radio that was playing in the mess tent, and I suspect we were one of the first to hear the news. I was not terribly surprised or concerned because we had been preparing for war and now it was here. I was not frightened by the news and remember going to bed and immediately falling asleep because the hour was very late. I know I would have been frightened if I had known what terrible destruction the Japanese had inflicted on our forces at Pearl Harbor. We never knew about our terrible losses until the war was over. I am sure our top brass knew, but we were never told, which I am sure was best.

I may not have been scared the night when I heard that the war had started, but I would be lying if I said I was not scared when the second night rolled around. The day started with an early frantic call (before breakfast) for all to immediately assemble in front of the first sergeant's tent. I had a pretty good idea of what it was all about, but most of the outfit had not yet heard.

Anyway, we were told that we were now at war with Japan and would be issued arms and ammunition. All morning long cases filled with rifles and pistols were opened and handed out to the troops, as well as a gas mask each. The rifles and pistols had been packed in cosmoline (a heavy grease), and it took a considerable amount of time to get them cleaned and operable. I was issued a .30 caliber Springfield rifle and a .45 caliber Colt automatic pistol.

Since we were Air Corp personnel, we had never received instructions on firing a rifle, and a lot of these men had never had a rifle in their hands before. A lot were like me, however. They were farm boys who were brought up with guns and knew how to use them.

For ammunition we were given one bandalier of rifle bullets and an extra clip of .45 caliber bullets. A bandalier was an ammunition holder made out of cloth that you hung around your neck. It had small pockets or sections that held a total of about twenty or twenty-five shells. These bandaliers were World War I vintage. It is interesting to know that bullets with lead slugs had been outlawed for war at the Geneva Convention, but here they were because it was all we had.

There were more modern ammunition supplies around, but not enough for everyone. I did manage to pick up some of the better stuff, plus some tracer bullets later on when I helped arm some of the planes. Eventually I was glad to have the old lead bullets, because they were very weak and came in handy later on for shooting birds and other small things like fish. They were about as strong as a .22 caliber long bullet, and did not tear up a bird when it was hit. Before I forget, I might mention that we were also issued emergency rations, which consisted of a can of corned beef and a pack of hard tack. Hard tack was a hard cracker. We were also given hard hats (steel helmets). Getting equipped and making our gear functional took the entire day.

★ 3 ★

The Enemy Comes

That night we all retired to our tents early because a total blackout was in effect. It really made no difference to us because we had no lights in the tents anyway. All of a sudden, around midnight or so, there was loud whistling on the outside by our first sergeant, the whistling followed by shouts of "Everyone up! Everyone up! Air raid!"

We could hear air-raid sirens in the background so we were sure it was the real thing.

A lot of the guys were up and dressed and out in minutes, but a lot were slow and lagging around. They figured it was a dry run so why hurry. Once out of the tents we were told to go to the edge of the jungle nearby and get away from our tents because they would undoubtedly be a target for the enemy.

Everyone did as he was told, but before long there was grumbling, and people wanted to get back to bed. Even though we stayed out about two hours everyone felt it was a dry run. The air-raid sirens had long stopped, and no enemy activity was observed by way of bombing or strafing. Eventually we were given the order to return to our tents and, needless to say, we were ready.

Once back in the dark tents we got out of our clothes, and before long everyone was sound asleep again. I am not sure how long we were asleep, but some time later that night we were awakened by horrendous sounds the likes of which we had never heard before. Great explosions were going on all around us, and the ground was shaking as if an earthquake was taking place. Brilliant flashes of light could be seen through the thick canvas of our tents.

By now our first sergeant was out again yelling for all to head for the jungle again. This time there were no stragglers. A lot of the guys just took off in their underwear, some had pants and no shirt, some a shirt but no pants.

I managed to get on clothes and (untied) shoes before leaving our tent, but once outside I was stunned for a while by what I heard and saw. The sky was filled with bursting anti-air-craft fire, and tracer bullets could be seen headed upward in all directions. The sound of straining aircraft could also be heard intermingled with the rumbling sound of exploding bombs. It looked like the world was coming to an end. Needless to say, I recovered from my astonishment in a hurry and passed up some slow pokes on the way to cover in the jungle.

We made a terrible mistake by not checking out the wooded area prior to our needing it. As we went tearing into the woods in the dark, we suddenly found ourselves suspended in air before landing in a tangle of vines and sticky briars. What we did not know, until now, was the presence of a twenty-to-thirty foot sheer drop off a short distance into the jungle. That is why there was still such thick woods so near Fort McKinley.

I think every last man went over this cliff, but luckily no one was seriously hurt. A lot of scratches and bruises, but no broken bones. The briars and vines and thick ground cover, actually helped break our fall. This is where we sat out the battle going on all around us, because there was nothing that we could do. Even after things quieted down no one returned to the tent area that night. We just curled up and slept on the floor of the jungle. War had now come to us with a bang, and it was real.

The bombings and strafings and sounds of war were to be repeated day after day, and we no longer ran for cover as we did that first night. During the first raids two of our men (16th Sqdn.) were hit by enemy fire. One was killed instantly and the other got a bullet through his shoulder from a strafing Jap plane, but he was actually one of the lucky ones, because he was sent to Australia and eventually back to the States.

We stayed around Fort McKinley a few more days, and I recall going to the PX to get more film for my camera. When I purchased the camera in Hawaii, I only bought two rolls of film. With the war now on I knew I would need more.

At the PX I told the clerk, a Filipino woman, that I would like several rolls of film. She went to check and came back and said that she had seven rolls in stock. I said I would take all seven, if she could sell them all to me. She said she could because they were on the verge of closing down the PX.

I remember reaching for my money in my pocket and in the process knocked my pistol out of its holster, and it went scooting across the floor. It startled other people around me and I really felt embarrassed because I knew that they were thinking: Who gave that guy a gun?

One night, while still at McKinley, I went with some of the guys to a place similar to a USO, where we could get something to drink and relax for a moment. It was not a club or anything like that but only a house completely blacked out from the outside and dimly lit on the inside by candles. It was not very far from our tent area and still on the base.

While sipping on a cold drink (non-alcohol) someone came rushing in, shouting that the Japs were dropping troops by parachute in the area. We had no reason to doubt him because we were warned that this was a possibility. We all grabbed our weapons and rushed outside ready to do battle. Instead of descending parachutes we found large puffs of smoke drifting away from where anti-aircraft guns were being fired. We still had a lot to learn.

By this time I suspect all or almost all of our aircraft had been destroyed on the ground, a fact that we were not aware of at this time. We were also not aware that our dive bombers, which we had last seen in Hawaii, had been diverted to Australia and would not dock in the Philippines. Knowing what I know now that may have been a good thing, because the chances are they would have been destroyed on the ground like the rest of our planes.

We soon got orders to pack our gear and head for the vicinity of a place called Lypa. I am not sure of this spelling, but the place was south of Manila and on the south side of the island of Luzon. We were to set up an airstrip and get ready to service airplanes that would soon arrive. I was foolish enough to believe that we were finally getting our planes. The air strip that we found was just that. A landing strip in the middle of a sugarcane field, similar to a landing strip that crop dusters use today. No hangars, no buildings, no power, nothing.

Anyway, we unloaded our gear in a nearby coconut grove which offered some shade. In the grove there were ripe coconuts stacked in piles man-high.

We thought that later on we might sample some of these since there was apparently no one around to object. I should point out that our original mission to the Philippines was to set up a base or airstrip on the island of Cebu, which is an island to the south of Luzon. Because the war apparently came sooner than expected our plans changed, and we wound up at Lypa.

Bivouacked in coconut grove at Lipa

We were not long at Lypa. In fact, we were still in the process of setting up camp when we got orders again to pack up as quickly as possible and head on back to Manila. I think we spent one night in Lypa.

By the time we had everything loaded the sun was going down, and darkness soon took over as we motored back to Manila. We were in a blackout mode and traveling was very slow because of it. I remember carefully lighting a cigar as I rode in the back of a truck, making sure that no excess light came from the lit match. I also recall that the cigar burned in a strange way. Instead of burning the tip completely as it was smoked it only burned on the inside leaving the outer side completely intact. I thought to myself this was a perfect blackout smoke, if the process could be made to repeat itself.

Talking about cigars, the ones in the Philippines were the best that I had ever run into, before or since. The variety or make that I am referring to, the name of which I cannot recall, was encased in four wrappers to keep it soft and fresh. Like everything else I was soon out of these cigars.

When we received word to pull out of Lypa, the reason given was that the Japanese had landed a few miles from us, and if we did not get out of there in a hurry we might be overrun. I look back now and think that the real story was that the Japs had landed in force and they, our commanders, wanted all of us evacuated to the Bataan Peninsula as quickly as possible.

As we approached Manila from the south in the dark, we could see huge fires burning throughout the city. Eventually we wound up at the docks of Manila where we found troops boarding boats to be shuttled to Bataan. Apparently there were not enough boats to handle everyone, because they called for volunteers to drive trucks and take troops around the bay to the Bataan Peninsula. All the troops and drivers that went this way were volunteers.

I was one of the volunteers even though we were told that we might encounter the Japanese ground troops before we got there.

Before taking off we loaded our trucks with all the food that they could hold plus a good supply of cigarettes. After everyone pulled out, the warehouses and all supplies remaining would be torched and destroyed before they fell into the hands of the enemy.

When we were ready to go, I could not find a seat in the trucks so I decided to ride atop the water trailer being pulled by one of the vehicles. I thought this would be a nice, cool ride on a hot night, but what a mistake that was.

As we rode along I was smothered in dust and besides my lungs and nose plugged up, my pants were covered with mud, and I had trouble holding on. What happened was that the water in the tank that I was riding on sweated, which then soaked my pants. The soaked pants then collected dust, which eventually turned into mud. I did not realize that the trip by truck was going to be so long, otherwise I would have found a better place to ride.

Some time later out of Manila our convoy abruptly stopped, and we could hear shouting up ahead. Our first impression was that we had run into the Japs, but that turned out not to be the reason.

Because we were traveling under blackout conditions, one of our trucks with a load of troops had run off the road and turned completely over in a deep ditch. The ditch was filled with water and deep, soft mud, and the guys were struggling to get out. Most were actually completely buried in mud and had we not pulled them out immediately they would have drowned or suffocated.

What saved them all was the fact that the water was shallow and the mud deep. When the truck nipped over instead of crushing people as it fell on them, it actually pushed them down in the soft mud. Many would have died, however, if we had not been there immediately to assist.

Eventually we got going again, and I jumped back on the water tank. Up to this time riding the water tank was miserable, but the worst was yet to come, as mentioned previously. At one time during the ride I almost fell asleep and my rifle almost fell from my hand. It was a struggle staying awake, because I was extremely tired and hungry, as our last meal was breakfast at Lypa.

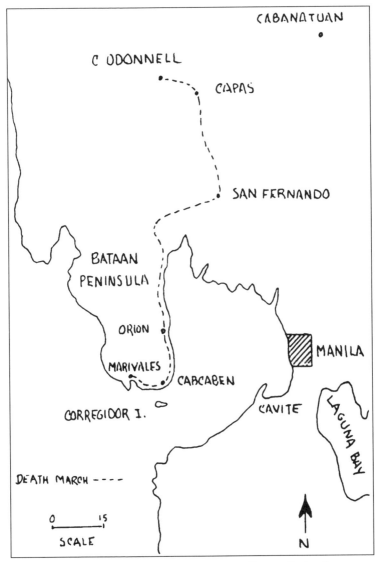

Enlarged portion of Luzon Island showing Bataan Peninsula

★ 4 ★

Arrival in Bataan

After a ride that seemed to last forever, we finally stopped at a small stream on the side of the road. Apparently we were now on the Bataan Peninsula and safe for the time being. It was early morning, and I recall we had sardines and crackers for breakfast. Someone also mentioned that it was Christmas Day.

Life had really taken on some excitement lately. Eighteen days after landing in the Philippine Islands war had broken out and I had had just about all the excitement that I could stand since. Little did I know that the worst by far was yet to come.

Later on that day we moved farther down the peninsula and eventually picked out a spot in the jungle where we stayed until overrun by the enemy. The location was several miles off the highway, in very thick jungle on the flanks of Mt. Bataan.

We were on a clear running stream and now well concealed from the enemy. To get where we were we had to make our own trail, yet we did not want it visible from the air.

We no longer had tents. I don't know whatever happened to them, but if they were still with us, I doubt if we would have ever used them. They would have given away our position to the enemy flying over. So without tents we had to make do by living in the open without shelter. Everyone picked out his spot and dug a foxhole, which was now standard practice wherever we went. I picked a spot right up against a towering tree with its root system that resembled flying buttresses. I notched two of these huge roots so that I

44

could set up two parallel saplings, which would become side pieces for my bed. The saplings were strong enough to support a person and were anchored in a horizontal position in the notched root system.

Next I wrapped heavy canvas between the parallel saplings and there was my bed. It was well down in between the huge roots and gave me excellent protection from flying shrapnel should bombs be dropped in the area.

To get to my foxhole I just had to roll out of my bed, and I fell right into it. When I finished my bunk I decided that I would try it by stretching out on it. I wiggled around a bit to see if it would hold me without breaking, when I was startled by eyes looking down on me. High up in my big sheltered tree were several monkeys, who apparently were watching me all the time.

After everyone had selected a place to stay, we built a shower at the river. I call it a river, but it was only a small stream, about three or four feet wide. The good thing about it was it was clean enough to drink and it ran constantly. The shower that I mentioned was made out of bamboo split from the huge variety that existed everywhere. This was our shower, and I must say a very fine one at that. It was also close enough to the galley to give water to the cooks.

As we turned off the main highway to our bivouac area, we noticed the U.S. Army Engineers were constructing a runway. It was in an area where one would not normally consider a runway to be. Huge trees had to be felled and pushed aside and boulders as large as an automobile had to be moved. It was well on its way, however, when we first saw it. The runway did not extend down to the highway but stopped short of it by about 100 yards. A few days later we found out that this is where we would be operating out of. The airstrip was now known as Cabcabin Field, named after a small barrio just down the road from it.

Since we had brought tons of food with us to Bataan, we ate like kings for a few days. We ate that way until the quartermaster came by and picked it all up. Apparently we were the only outfit that did this and now we had to share with those that came with nothing. They let us keep our cigarettes, however.

Besides bringing food we also brought all of our tools for working on airplanes. This was the best thing that ever happened to us and because of it we were assigned to take care of the few remaining planes. Other outfits dropped everything and ran when they were told to evacuate to Bataan, but we packed everything that we had and took it with us. As I recall we wound up with seven or eight P40s and a couple of other small planes and that was it.

At first I was assigned to dig revetments for the planes, and later on was on a machine gun at the field. The airplanes were not left at the field but pulled high in the hills and concealed under the heavy forest canopy. Here they were lowered in wheel trenches until their wings practically touched the ground. Then they were surrounded by sandbags and covered with brush. The Japanese never did spot them, because they were never bombed or strafed.

We had some dummies set up at the field, however, which they bombed constantly. Later on we had some of our wrecked planes, which we also used as decoys. The planes were wrecked by our own pilots as they tried to take off on the narrow runway.

I mentioned earlier the huge boulders lining the runway. This was our problem. A P40 airplane did not have what is called a tricycle landing gear. It had the two front wheels and a small tail wheel, which meant that on the ground its nose was sticking up and its tail down.

The nose stuck up to the point where the pilot could not see the runway until his plane reached enough speed to bring the nose down. In many cases this was too late. Unless the plane was perfectly lined up with the runway it would crash in the rocks before it got off the ground. We never lost one of our planes on Bataan from enemy fire, but did lose all but about three while trying to take off. The pilots were not afraid to fly, but they were scared to take off.

We were not able to put our planes up every day because fuel was rationed. We would have to wait several days before we got enough to put one in the sky. We only put up one at a time for the most part, because all they were primarily going up for was reconnaissance. They were not supposed to fight unless it was absolutely necessary. Sooner or later when they went up Jap Zero fighters would be after them. Their counter-measure, if possible, was to go into a steep dive for Corregidor where our antiaircraft fire there would drive the Japs off.

It seemed like our field got bombed just about every day, and it was especially heavy after we sent a plane up. The Japanese would bomb the runway and the dummies on the side and then stop for a while. I believe they stopped because they thought that they had destroyed everything that we had.

Lo and behold to the surprise of the Japs, here would come another American plane off of that same runway. It finally got to the point where it was almost impossible to get a plane off without it being bombed as it was taking off.

Mount Bataan was always covered with clouds at its crest and the Japs hung out in these clouds waiting for our planes. I later found what was surely the location of their spotter high in the mountains when I was on one of my hunting trips.

At the start of the war, bombs frightened the devil out of me. I figured there was no way that I could survive so many close calls day after day. There was many a day when bombs fell within 20 or 30 feet of me and eventually some much closer. If it had not been for strategically located foxholes, I know I would not be here today. One day, however, something happened that caused me to change my pessimistic outlook.

I was on a machine gun at the field, and all was quiet. I was out of my pit staring at things on the ground when I noticed an ant running back and forth. Just to have something to do I picked up pieces of rock and dirt about Ping-Pong ball size and started throwing them at the ant. After several misses, I picked up larger pieces to throw, but still continued to miss. It soon dawned on me that my chances of hitting the ant were very slim so I stopped throwing.

It is strange but this experience I equated with the bombs that were aimed at me constantly, and I then realized that I was probably as hard to hit as that ant.

I mentioned that the bombs were aimed at me. I know that they were not all aimed at me, but I think everyone in a bombing raid has that feeling.

The closest that I came to being hit was one day at the airstrip when I was watching an Army engineer patching up the bombed runway. He was on a grader like you normally see working on roads in the States.

All of a sudden Jap planes came tearing out of the clouds, and we started heading for cover. By we, I mean the guy on the grader and myself. At the last minute we found ourselves heading for the same foxhole and since he was slightly ahead, I let him have it and went for one a few feet farther.

Just as I dove in feet first the bombs were on us. My left arm got peppered with shrapnel, and I was almost covered with falling rocks and dirt. My clothes were almost ripped from my body by the concussion, but I survived again because the bombing was now over.

The reason my left hand and arm were hit was because as I jumped into the foxhole I almost lost my steel helmet. When I reached up to keep it on my head apparently my hand and arm were above ground level and out of the foxhole.

When I finally stood up and looked around I saw a large smoking crater in the exact spot where the other person's foxhole was. He had suffered a direct hit and died instantly. I looked around to see if I could find the body, but found nothing. He was apparently blown to pieces, or his body thrown far from the explosion.

One thing that I did find, however, was a U.S. Army Engineer compass. I picked it up and put it in my pocket hoping to give it to some of his buddies, which never happened.

The war was almost over for us, and I don't recall getting

Author is slightly wounded by exploding bomb, which killed American soldier in nearby foxhole

back down to the airstrip after this. My wounds were really insignificant but enough to eventually get me a Purple Heart. More about the compass later.

During a bombing raid I would normally peep over the edge of my foxhole to see where the planes were. At first all you knew was that they were headed in your direction, and you had better stay put. As they got closer and closer you could now tell better if they were going to pass to the side of you, or if they were coming directly over.

If they were directly overhead you began to sweat because that meant you were about to take a pounding. As you watched the planes you could all of a sudden see many small flashes of silver appear just below the planes. This meant that their bombs had been dropped, and they were on their way down. These silver flashes were only visible for a few seconds and then disappeared.

If you were still looking up, the next thing you saw—now heard—were these large black objects coming right at you with a terrible hissing sound. In a fraction of a second they were exploding with a terrific bang as they hit the ground. They did not go off simultaneously but one at a time until they had all exploded.

If the bombs were just in front of you, you could hear them getting closer and closer and that was the scary part. It wasn't until you could hear the explosions go past you, that you knew you were safe and could now relax. That's when you thanked God for foxholes.

I mentioned earlier that I was on a .50-caliber machine gun at the airstrip, which is why I was around so much bombing. The machine guns were some that had been taken from crashed airplanes. We were set up right next to the runway on both sides. As I recall we had two or three pits. We were not terribly effective, and I do not remember ever knocking down a Japanese plane.

As the enemy planes dove down low over the field to drop their bombs, you would start firing, and you could swear, from the tracer bullets, that bullets were hitting home, but the planes did not fall. There was an antiaircraft battery near the field for a while, and I did see them knock down a plane with their 20-millimeter gun. Seems like I heard that some of the relief guys on our .50-caliber guns did knock down another Jap, but I did not see it.

Besides bombs and enemy strafing there was another danger coming from the air. It was the hot, whistling metal fragments raining down on us from our own antiaircraft guns at Corregidor.

In machine-gun position at Cabcabin Field

We were right across from Corregidor Island and witnessed and heard all of the action taking place there. They received extremely heavy bombing day after day. The purpose of the bombing was to try to wipe out the remaining planes that we had on the ground or tear up the runway so that they could not get off the ground.

It wasn't long before our food supply was practically gone, and we had to scrounge around to find something to eat. By now all of the bananas and coconuts were gone, and we started on the caribou or any other meat that we could find. We eventually ate all of our horses that belonged to the cavalry and the mules that were used to pull their cannons.

I will never forget when our mess sergeant returned from the quartermasters' with the hind quarter of a mule. It still had its hairy skin on as well as its hoof. I would have been better off had I not seen this, because that evening with every bite that I took I could see that old mule.

I say old, since chewing it was impossible. The meat was in a stew, cut up in small cubes, so that you could swallow them without having to chew. Horse meat was good, but caribou was about as tough as mule.

Every chance that I had I hunted the jungle for food. My main pursuit was the wild boar that was found locally. I did manage to bring in a small one for the kitchen once, but the large ones were more lucky in eluding me.

I normally hunted alone, but one time I had a friend with me, which turned out to be a mistake. The jungle was so thick with sticky briers and other plants that the only way you could get through it was by walking up or down river beds. Most of the streams were lined with various sized boulders, and it was on these that you traveled.

This particular day we were trying to cross over a stream by way of a large fallen tree when two enormous boars rushed out from underneath us. They started to immediately climb to the brush lining the stream instead of following the rocky river path. I was startled for a second but soon had my rifle on one when the guy with me shouted, "Don't shoot, don't shoot."

I lowered my rifle to see why not, and the pigs disappeared. I wanted to know why he did not want me to shoot, because he knew as well as I that was why we were out. He had no explanation for saying what he did.

As I look back now he probably was afraid that our rifle fire would attract the enemy. There were many snipers around, and several of our troops were killed by them so I guess he had reason to do what he did.

I never did run into a sniper while hunting, but I did find where I think an enemy spotter hid out. This was high up on Mt. Bataan, an area that I covered extensively while hunting.

I came across a large tree with freshly dug dirt all around it. Right away I thought, animal, food, but as I circled the tree and poked around I could not find where the dirt had come from.

About that time I noticed dirt caught on some of the branches higher up. The living part of this tree was actually a large strangling fig that had taken over an exceptionally large mahogany tree, which it had killed.

If you ever have been around a strangling fig you know how easy they are to climb. The dirt high up on the branches suggested to me that this was done by man so I started to climb. As I got near the top—twenty- to twenty-five feet off the ground—I looked down and could clearly see our runway several thousand feet away.

I still had not actually connected this with anything until I reached the top and looked down into this large hollow tree. Immediately I could see that it had been lived in and that is when it hit me. Undoubtedly this was a lookout point for the Japanese spying on our airstrip and that is when I pulled my head back as quickly as I could.

I thought to myself, What a foolish mistake, as I slowly climbed back to the ground. I did not see anyone in the tree, but a person could have easily been hiding in one of the side roots. Someone could have easily blown off my head. I was going to return later with help, but the war was nearly over for us. I never did get to return.

I will now tell you why I hunted alone. I was out one day with this guy who wanted to hunt with me because I had killed a pig. I said OK, so we took off and headed up a small creek not terribly far from camp.

We were slowly making our way from rock to rock, trying to be as quiet as possible when I heard something and turned around. The sound was from small pebbles and dirt falling from the side of this fairly steep channel wall. The wall was about fifteen to twenty feet high, and as I searched to find what was causing the disturbance I spotted it.

An extremely large snake, pretty well hidden in the thick growth of vegetation and roots and starting to move. When the guy with me saw it he took off as fast as he could and left me with it alone.

I saw it as a huge meal for everyone and decided to kill it. I could never find its head and about that time it started to move up and away and that is when I shot. The shot hit somewhere in its body but it kept going. This is when I should have had a more powerful shell. The snake was either a boa constrictor or a python, but I am not sure which is found in the Philippines. It was huge.

There were some wild chickens that lived in the jungle near our camp area and as hard as I tried to get one for a meal I never succeeded. I imagine they are still there or, if not them, at least their descendants.

I have never seen a bird as wild as a wild chicken. Even though I knew exactly where they lived I could never creep up on them without first being seen. Once they saw you they were gone.

Another time when I was hunting alone, I had taken a position on a large rock in the middle of a small stream waiting for wild pigs, when I heard something coming upstream. I slowly raised my rifle and pointed it in the direction of the noise waiting for what I thought would be a pig to appear.

Instead of a pig, what appeared over my rifle barrel was an American officer. He didn't know how close he came to being shot. He finally spotted me, but I had already lowered my rifle.

Talking about people in the woods, there was a person in the outfit that was so frightened by the war that during the day he moved slightly away from our camp and slept under bushes in the jungle. His only job was to dig slit trenches (latrines) and when this was accomplished he disappeared in the jungle and only reappeared at night. I found him on several occasions while hunting.

The comment about slit trenches brings up another good story, and this one is on me. This happened the first day we pitched camp. I had to use the slit trench and as you probably guessed they were hidden in the bushes and some distance from our living area. As I squatted there with my pants down I heard something coming through the bushes. Before I could get my pants up and reach for my rifle, the head of this monstrous lizard appeared. It scared the daylights out of me because I did not know if it would attack and bite or what.

Anyway, I slowly reached for a clump of dirt and threw it at the creature, which sent it scurrying through the underbrush. It, of course, was an iguana, which was the first that I had ever seen.

There was a large sunken ship in the bay not far from the end of our runway. One day a friend and I decided to investigate it, which meant leaving our jungle cover and walking on an open beach.

Jap planes were constantly flying around the area, apparently for the purpose of reconnaissance. The Japs never dropped bombs or tried to strafe anyone so we generally ignored them.

That day, however, apparently the mission had been changed, because before we knew what was happening a plane was coming down on us. A single bomb was released, which fell in the water some distance away. From then on we were more cautious about exposing ourselves.

During our stay on Bataan each outfit had a particular part of the beach to defend. We were to defend a portion that faced Manila Bay. Since we were supposed to keep the

Cabcabin Field being attacked by Japanese dive-bomber

enemy from landing on that particular area we, of course, investigated the spot.

We determined where our machine gun would be, where our rifle men would be, etc.

We also picked out a spot for our command post which was quite some distance removed from any fighting that might occur. I had to pay special attention to this location because I was designated runner for the outfit. Since we had no phone or rapid capabilities to communicate, orders and commands, etc. had to be transmitted by word of mouth.

I did not ask or volunteer for this job but did feel that I was highly qualified because of my forays through the jungle.

This job turned out to be more than I had expected, however. The first time we went out to reconnoiter I made a mental picture of the location and direction of our command post and felt that I would have no trouble finding it if the need ever arose.

Well, the need did arise, because one night we were called out as it appeared that the Japanese were sending landing crafts across the bay.

We rushed down to our positions and got ready for a landing that never came. When it appeared that nothing was going to happen, I was instructed to notify our command post that the recommendation from the field was that we should give up our positions and head in.

I remember thinking, You've got to be kidding, but they weren't. So I started out in the general direction of where I thought I should head without a light.

Luckily the night was not pitch dark. A partial moon did present some light, allowing for some vision, but I am amazed that to this day I am still not lost somewhere in that jungle. I fell into briers and slipped over rocks and logs, stumbled through water, and really did not think I would make it.

I don't know how long it took or how I ever managed, but I finally reached our command post looking like I had just had a ferocious battle and lost.

I passed on my message and thought, If they want me to return with a message, they can get lost because I am not about to try that route again. Luckily this was my first and only time that my services as a runner were used.

Although we never had to defend our beach position, several, I should say many, of the men in my outfit did see hard and severe fighting in areas where the Japanese had made landings behind our front lines. Although we were Air Corps, we were ultimately designated as infantry and carried on and fought as such.

When the front lines were active we could always hear the roar of the canons being fired and the noise of the resulting explosions. Many a night I fell asleep listening to this noise and especially during the last few weeks and days of our struggle. With this noise getting closer and closer as the front lines fell back, I never in my wildest dreams felt that we would be defeated. We were tired, hungry and in many cases sick, but we were still ready to fight.

One day stray soldiers started appearing at our airstrip, and this surprised me because I had never seen this before. In talking to them they said that they had left the front line looking for food. They were being constantly bombarded by Japanese guns and no food was getting to them. It was either go out and look, for food or starve to death.

I don't want to imply that this was done by everyone. Our men were staying put, hungry as they were. It is easy to see now how the Japanese were able to eventually overrun our position.

One day we got word that the monsoon season would soon be starting and to keep from getting wet, when the rains came, we should build a cover over our bunk. So I grabbed an ax and headed for a place in the jungle where I could chop down small trees without giving away our position.

I got about two hundred yards or so from camp when I spotted what looked like a good tree for making a roof support. I gave the tree one blow with my ax, and I knew I had discovered a gold mine.

The tree was a sassafras. I recognized the odor immediately. Needless to say, I did not cut the tree down, but, instead, carefully dug up some of its roots.

After I had a good handful, I carefully covered the area that I had disturbed with leaves and brush. The cut that I made to the trunk of the tree was also easily concealed. I was periodically going to furnish our cook with enough roots so that everyone in the outfit would have tea, but I did not want anyone to know where the tree was. It would have been ravaged in days.

Only one person in my outfit tried to get me to show him where the tree was, but I would not. This was one of the officers. I did consent to get some leaves for him, which he showed to some Negritos who lived nearby.

He wanted to know if they knew this tree, and they said no. So he sent them looking for one, but they were never successful. They did not find mine or another like it.

The Negritos were small, black native people who lived in the jungle. They survived mainly by hunting and fishing, but did have a small cleared area in the forest, where they raised a few vegetables and some hogs and chickens.

They were also expert locators of beehives, which kept them well supplied with honey. I learned their method, but never had the time or patience to have it succeed for me.

They did it by watching a bee take off after feeding. They discovered that a bee heads straight for its hive once it is full. All you have to do is follow the bee by sight as far as you can see. Move to that last place of sighting, wait for the next bee to come by and watch it as long as you can, repeat, repeat, etc. and you finally come to the hive.

Most of the time everyone went about his duties without a word of dissent or grumbling, but one activity had everyone furious. After working all night in the field or all night on a machine gun, we would come into camp hoping to get some rest, but one of our officers had a different idea.

Instead of getting much needed and deserved rest, he had us out digging a cave, of all things. Digging a foxhole in this area was bad enough, but now he had us digging a cave in solid rock. After digging for several weeks we had a hole about six feet high, six or seven feet wide and possibly 15 to 20 feet deep into the face of this rock cliff. We tried to tell him that this would be no protection from a bomb. If one fell at the entrance, it would kill us all. That did not register with him because we continued to dig.

The guy was a coward and wanted a place to run and hide if things got rough. Someone made a crude sign that said, " 's Folly." I won't give his name because I am not sure if he survived the war or not.

One night I had a pretty good scare that turned out to be nothing. I was awakened by a terrific storm with high winds, very heavy lightning, rumbling thunder and much rain.

A few seconds after I awoke there was a brilliant flash of lightning and an immediate boom of thunder followed by the crash of a large tree. It was so close that I instinctively ducked even though I was in bed. It was close, close, close and I knew it.

When I figured the tree had fallen as far to the ground as it could I decided to get up to see what damage had occurred.

Remember it was dark, but I decided anyway to have a look just in case the tree fell on someone. As I started to get out of bed I was blocked by a solid object—an enormous tree. The hair stood up on my head, because I immediately realized that the fallen tree had missed me by inches.

Thinking I was trapped, I decided to slip out of my bunk on the tree side that my bed was attached to. That is when I realized what had happened. In my state of confusion I had tried to get out of my bunk on the wrong side—the side where a large tree always existed. My tree.

You may recall earlier that I said our runway, or airstrip, did not go quite to the road. Well, one day we got word that large bombers would be available to help us out if we enlarged the runway. This sounded like good news, so we were given axes and shovels and bolo knives and started hacking away at the jungle.

We worked like dogs from sunup to sundown for days and finally lengthened the landing strip in both directions, but all in vain. We never did get planes; today I know that none were ever intended to reach us.

The jungle had ants all over it—on the ground, up in the trees. You name it and there they were. I will never forget what happened to one poor guy who was helping on the runway. He started to chop down a tree, not realizing that a huge ant's nest was just above his head. Ants by the hundreds fell on top of him. I am sure that if we hadn't been around to help, he possibly could have been killed by them. They were very large, ferocious ants.

Another time while I was silently sitting on a rock hoping

that a wild boar would come by, I noticed a bunch of ants nearby that appeared to be extremely excited for some reason. They were sitting on top of this rock, and their antennas were moving vigorously.

I could not imagine why they appeared so excited until I saw a large lizard approaching below the rock that they were on. When the lizard was finally beneath them they piled offten masse and in seconds had their victim completely covered. There was a furious thrashing, but to no avail. In short order the lizard was dead, and the ants started to drag it off. I had never seen ants hunt like this before.

The runway that we finally extended even had makeshift landing lights, because we thought that our planes would be coming in at night, since the Japanese were not in the air then.

One night we turned on the lights (the first and only time that I recall) for one of our planes to come in. It landed without any trouble and was piloted by an American with a single passenger. I don't know what kind of plane it was, but it was obviously not a fighter. Supposedly the passenger of the plane was a British officer who had come to Bataan to find out why our antiaircraft fire was so effective.

Apparently the British, wherever they were, were not doing as well as we were. They hung around for a while, and when we got the word that they were ready to leave turned the airstrip lights on again. With the lights on they took off immediately and once in the air, off went the lights.

About fifteen or twenty minutes later we heard an airplane in the air, fairly low, circling back and forth over our strip. We were not sure who it was, but felt that it must be a Jap trying to get us to turn on the landing lights again so that he could clobber us. We were not going to fall for it so the lights stayed off.

After circling around a bit longer the plane dropped down real low like it was coming in for a landing. It landed all right but crosswise to the runway, which was a big mistake.

It crashed into the huge boulders that lined the runway on both sides and went skidding into the bush with pieces of plane flying in all directions.

We rushed out to the wreckage expecting to see probably dead Japanese and found instead the American and British officer, who had just left a short while before.

Luckily, they were both alive and not seriously hurt. They were fortunate in that when the plane hit the ground it broke up with the fuselage and engine going in one direction and the wings and ruptured gas tanks going in another. Because of this, there was no fire, which was a big plus in their favor as far as their survival was concerned.

They were coming back because they thought that they were having engine trouble when in fact they were not. It appears that the plane was British and the instruments were metric, which the American misread.

While in the tropics I learned something about bananas. When we first evacuated to Bataan there were numerous banana plants around and many loaded with fruit. They were, of course, green and looked fully mature, so I gathered a bunch and took them back to camp.

Thinking that they needed to be kept cool and in the dark to ripen, I put them in my foxhole and covered them with leaves. Every few days I would look to see how they were doing, but nothing was happening. They were as green as ever.

After a few weeks I figured they would never ripen so I threw them out, possibly for the hogs. Several days later I went to see if hogs had been around to eat them and found that they were beautifully ripened. I picked them all up again and ate until it hurt.

If I had known that to ripen bananas you do the opposite of what I did, I could have ripened a few at a time and made them last much longer. Before long there were no more bananas to be had. In fact, there were no more plants because we ate them, too. We ate the center of the stalks, which was like celery.

One day we got word to gas up the last P40s that we had (three as I recall) and get them ready for takeoff. We pulled them out of their hiding place in the jungle and down to the field, where the pilots were waiting.

Normally the pilots wanted to jump in and take off immediately before the Japs saw them, but this time it was different. They said that they were leaving Bataan and going to a field on one of the islands to the south which was still in friendly hands.

Before the pilot got in his plane, he asked me and a friend of mine if we wanted to send a message home. We said yes because this was the first opportunity that we had to do so since leaving the States.

He had a pad and pencil, and I wrote a short note letting everyone at home know that I was well. I really did not expect it to get home, but it did.

It was sent from the island of Cebu (where we were originally scheduled to go) and when the island of Luzon fell my family did not know that I was on it. They thought that I was on Cebu because of the note. When all of the Philippine Islands fell they then did not know what had happened to me.

When the last of our planes left, that was the beginning of the end. It may have been the same day or the day after that we were hurriedly taken back into camp and told to pack up. We were only to bring bare essentials. The clothes and shoes that we had on, tooth brushes, etc. Nothing else.

Of course, bare essentials included our arms and ammunition. We were also issued our emergency food supply and told that we could eat it then, which we did.

The emergency rations were a can of corned beef and a pack of hardtack, a cracker about as hard as a brick. This was the last American food that I had for three and-one-half years.

Since we were told that we were not coming back, and I could not take it with me, I buried all my other personal belongings in my foxhole. These personal items included all the exposed film that I had taken (but not my camera, which I took) plus a diary that I had kept during the war. It also included my high-school graduation ring. All of these items were placed in a wooden ammunition box and covered with dirt and debris. I figured I would be back.

After everyone was loaded on trucks we discovered that some of our men were missing. Come to find out, some had been apparently left at the field so we had to send a truck down for them. On the way out we were not going that way.

We also discovered another person missing, and since we knew that he had been deathly sick and could hardly walk, we went looking for him. He was eventually found lying on the ground under some bushes. He wanted us to take off without him, but we didn't.

By the time we finally pulled out, it was getting dark. The people that we got from the field said that they could hear Jap tanks coming up the road near where they were.

For the last several days the war had gotten much closer to us. Gunfire was almost constant, and at night you could see the flash of our cannons and hear exploding shells of the enemy. They were that close, but for some reason I was not afraid. Had I known the real situation, I am sure that I would have been greatly concerned. I thought that the Japs were just pushing us a little farther south, and we were giving up our position to form another front line closer to Corregidor.

When we finally were ready to leave, I jumped on the right front fender of one of our trucks and we took off. Traveling was extremely slow, because we were again moving under blackout conditions, and the road that we were on was nothing more than a trail that had been hacked through the jungle. Somewhere down the trail we must have intersected the main road, because we ran into a terrible traffic jam. Apparently a lot of other people were doing the same thing because we were all headed in the same direction, some in trucks and some on foot.

Traveling now was slower than ever. By now our big guns

on Corregidor were shooting at the Japs over our heads. By then they had apparently realized that they could blast the Japanese in the areas we had just vacated. These big shells sounded like a freight train going over.

When they started shooting, I knew that I was right in that we were moving under the protection of Corregidor's guns and would now be safe. Apparently it was hard to convince me that we were losing this fight.

Sometime during the night the moving column on the road stopped, and we were told it was to give our engineers time to vacate a portion of the road so that they could blow up an ammunition dump. It wasn't long before the sky lit up followed by a thunderous explosion. It was more than we expected and explosions continued for quite some time before we were allowed to continue.

I don't remember for sure if this happened before or after the ammunition dump was set off. In any event I was sitting on the fender of our truck when the whole thing began to sway back and forth. My first thought was that it was the people in the truck causing the movement so I jumped down on the ground and had the surprise of my life. It was the ground moving, which in turn was moving the truck. That was my first experience with an earthquake.

Shortly before daybreak we pulled up before a place that had real buildings (not nipa huts) and a nice open field nearby. We stopped and were told to find any place that we liked and get some rest. There were many, many other troops around and some already had small fires going. It appeared they were boiling water in tin cans to make coffee or what have you.

That made me think of the last coffee that I had. It was shortly after we arrived on Bataan. I managed to get some used coffee from our kitchen, and I would reuse it until my coffee would look like weak tea. At that point I would reparch the grinds and start over. Toward the end, of the coffee that is, it tasted more like charcoal water than coffee.

Another coffee story shortly, but I'm now reminded about

what happened when the cook gave me a slice of bread one night. It was three or four o'clock in the morning, and I had just returned from being relieved from my gun position at the field. To get to my bunk I had to pass near the kitchen. There was already someone there so I dropped in to see who it was. It was the cook getting ready for breakfast. He had already sliced some bread and was cooking white gravy which, by now, was what we were down to.

He offered me a slice of bread, and I was most grateful, but instead of eating it then, I decided that I would keep it until morning when breakfast would be served. I would then have gravy over two pieces of bread.

Since morning was not far off, I decided to stay dressed as I stretched out on my bed. I also left my shoes on. My bread was safely placed in my pocket. I had not fallen asleep yet when I felt something on my feet. I wasn't sure what it was, but I changed my position, and it was gone.

The minute I would settle down it would be back and it was no longer it but they. They were coming from all directions, and I had to jump up. When my eyes finally adjusted I saw that it was big rats, and they were after my bread. I could not get rid of them so I was forced to eat it before they would leave.

The place that we had stopped for rest after our night's ordeal was Marivales. It was a military base of some kind for the Marines before the war. After the war started I am not sure what it was used for.

With the large concentration of American troops on the ground, and many in the open, it was not long before the Japanese starting strafing us from the air. To keep from being hit, some of us decided to go inside one of the buildings, where it appeared we would be safe from enemy fire.

We were surprised to find inside real beds and mattresses that were not being used because there were no sheets or pillows around. Except for the beds, the place was bare.

The first thing we did was place the sick person on one of the bunks, and we all stretched out on others. The sick person was the one that we found in the bushes when we pulled out of our camp area the previous evening.

Before we could even relax, the Jap planes were back again, and bullets were coming into the building and ricocheting off the walls, floor, etc.

This did not seem like a safe place so we hastily got out of there and headed for the woods where we thought it would be much safer.

One of the guys had scrounged around and found some real coffee so, once under cover of trees and about 100 yards or so away from the buildings, we built a small fire and started boiling water.

The water was in a gallon tin can that we found nearby. Since the water had yet to boil, and I still had my camera around my neck, I decided to take another picture.

My camera had an automatic shutter, so we jumped in a foxhole nearby, stuck our heads out, heard the camera click, and there it was. This was the last picture that I would take, but there is more to the story.

Many years later, a friend of mine who was also in the picture, asked me if I had seen our picture in such and such a book, but I said I had not because I was not reading anything pertaining to Bataan. He kept telling me about it time after time, but I was not interested until I finally bought a book that was about the death march and sure enough, there it was. There was no doubt about it. Apparently the Japanese found my camera and developed the film that was in it. It is possible other pictures will surface someday, somewhere.

After taking the picture we got back out of the foxhole and sat around waiting for our water to boil.

We were not the only people under cover where we were. There were two officers not very far from us eyeing our coffee as hard as we were, but not saying a thing.

It wasn't long before we could hear the drone of Jap bombers coming from a distance. We looked up and sure enough there they were and headed our way.

As I remember there were about eight or ten of them,

and even though they were coming in a direction that would put them directly over us, we still sat around the fire waiting for our water to boil.

In the meantime, I noticed the two officers were already in a foxhole; I thought, Don't they know that those bombers are going after Corregidor?

Corregidor was just across from us, and it had been taking a pounding from the air for days. This, we felt, was another one of those raids.

Pretty soon we heard one of the officers say, "You better get under cover, guys," or words to that effect.

Since they were officers, we reluctantly obliged and slowly crawled back into the foxhole, where our picture was taken. It did not take us long to realize that we were wrong, and the officers were right because all of a sudden we could hear the swooshing of falling bombs. They started exploding as they hit the ground, and each explosion kept getting closer and closer, working in our direction.

I knew that we were in big trouble when I heard explosions getting louder and louder, then almost immediately we were practically obliterated by an exploding bomb that missed us by a few feet. When the bomb went off it sent dirt and large rocks flying in the air in all directions, and we were almost covered by falling debris.

This bomb was actually closer to me than the other bomb that killed the engineer on our airstrip and peppered my arm with shrapnel. You could reach out from our foxhole and practically touch the edge of the large crater that it made, but none of us was seriously hurt.

One of the men received a pretty good gash on his head when a large rock fell on him. Luckily he had on his steel helmet, or I should have said, my steel helmet. When we got into the foxhole, he inadvertently picked up my helmet, and I got his. I wound up with a dented head piece, but not the wound that went with it.

After it was over the officers looked at us as though to say, "I told you so," but never said a word.

That is when we decided that we had better go back and find our outfit. We never had that cup of java because the coffee was sent sky high and is probably still dripping down.

When we did find our outfit, we were flabbergasted by the news. We were surrendering. I could not believe it; all these men still with arms, and now, under the protection of Corregidor's big guns, we were giving up. But it was true.

We were told to destroy all of our weapons and ammunition immediately in any way that we could. Most people were disassembling their rifles and pistols and throwing them in the bay, so I did the same. It was the quickest way to get rid of them. I did not mind getting rid of my rifle, but I hated to throw away my pistol.

I was originally issued a .45 automatic, but later traded it with someone for a revolver. We had no way of keeping our weapons as clean as they should be, and it was a known fact that sometimes automatics would jam and not fire. I knew that a revolver would not, so that is why I traded. The only time that I ever fired either pistol was when a low-flying aircraft came by, and I did not have my rifle handy.

Now I wondered what to do with my camera. I was not about to throw it in the water, because I felt that someday I might get back and retrieve it. I looked around for a good hiding place, but could not find one so I stuck it under a bunch of roof slate that was piled nearby. I figured the slate night keep it dry, and if no one found it, it would last a long time. I also hated to lose the last roll of film that I had in the camera, because I had pictures of our last planes leaving, our hasty retreat from our camp, and the mass confusion that existed around us at the moment. But the camera was found by the Japanese; the proof of this surfaced in a picture published many years later.

We were told by our leaders to stay put until the Japs came in, and when they did we would be taken to prisoner-of-war camps, where we would sit out the rest of the war.

I did not like this idea at all, but you could tell that a lot of guys felt relieved. They were dirty, tired, hungry, and had

had enough of war. They felt now that they had survived and would soon be fed, sheltered and given some long-needed rest. Little did we know that we were headed for Hell.

Apparently a lot of the troops decided that instead of being captured they would take off for the jungle, which is what they did. Some, or I should say many, crossed over to Corregidor. Both decisions were a mistake.

Those that took off for the hills eventually turned themselves in later to the Japanese because they could not survive where they were. They could find nothing to eat, because everything on Bataan was already eaten or killed and malaria was making them too sick to fend for themselves. Those that reached Corregidor eventually got food, but had to survive the war that raged on for them for another month.

I said that those that fled made a mistake, but as I now look back and consider it, I may be wrong because they did not have to make the long, grueling march out of Bataan. Their chances of survival were probably better than ours. I got to talk later to one of the men who had fled to the hills but later turned himself in. He also had some horrible stories to tell-too horrible to write about here.

After getting rid of all of our weapons, we expected the Japs to appear at any moment, but that was not to be that day. That night we slept on the ground again, and by now we were becoming very hungry, not that we were not always hungry.

The last food that we had was the emergency rations that we ate when we broke camp the night before. We did not get much real rest that night because there was much milling around by the troops. There was constant talk going on during the night, but all you could see was the occasional flare from a match being struck to light a cigarette.

Next morning there were still no Japanese around us on the ground, but planes were still buzzing us from the air. They were up there, but this time not bombing and strafing us.

A pair of American officers were looking for someone to

go with them up the road to see if we could make contact with them. I jumped at the opportunity. The officers were in a jeep and since my poor sick buddy was with me (I should say us, because there were three of us), he was placed on the back seat where he could lie down. I rode on the fender again, my favorite spot it seems.

We took off going west out of Marivales on the main highway. A white rag was tied to a pole that we had sticking up from the jeep. We were not far down the road when a Jap plane made a dive for us, but we were told to stay put and not run.

Luckily the Jap did not shoot, but he pulled up, banked his plane around and came for us again. It was hard not to jump off the jeep and run, but we did not. We went up the road a bit farther and eventually turned around. We did not contact the Japanese, and the officers felt that this effort was too risky to continue. The next plane that came around may not be so kind. Since all officers had removed their insignias during the war, I never did know who the officers in the jeep were nor their rank.

By the time we got back to the group, Japanese troops had arrived from the other direction. They were already lining people up to count us. I jumped off the jeep and worked my way to the back of the group. Eventually they had us all lined up in military fashion and were barking out orders, which no one understood.

I was in the last group of men in the back. I was also the end man on the front row.

Pretty soon a Jap soldier came up to me muttering something and at the same time flapping his hand up and down. I looked at him with a puzzled look, because I didn't have the slightest idea what he wanted. The Jap kept up his puzzling gestures, and I could tell that he was getting more furious by the minute.

I turned around, looked at some of the guys and shrugged my shoulders indicating that I did not know what the Jap wanted.

Someone said, "He wants you to sit down." So I sat down and immediately received a crack across my head with a rifle butt. I knew then that that was not what he wanted so I immediately got back up. That is when he came and gave me a shove, and the guy next to me a shove and so on. He wanted us to start walking.

That was the beginning of our march out of Bataan, and I believe that I was the first one to start it, at least out from Marivales.

Bataan falls to the Japanese

★ 5 ★

March Out of Bataan

This is where my story is going to be more difficult to tell for two reasons. The first being that we were told, on our return to the U.S., that we were not to speak to anyone about our experience as prisoners of war-not the press, our families, friends. The reason for this was that somewhere down the line we might be in a war again, and undoubtedly more prisoners would be taken.

If we revealed how we survived, this information would get in the hands of our enemy, which then would make it doubly tough on our prisoners. This made very good sense, and I did abide by it. Over the years, however, our story has been told many times so now I feel free to tell mine.

The second reason that I was, and still am, reluctant to tell about my experiences as a POW is the fact that I thought it would be impossible to describe what we went through. Impossible to tell and impossible to describe by written word. I have since read many good books on the subject and seen film documentaries made, but you had to be there and experience it to know what it was like. I know that my meager attempt will also fail, but I will write about it anyway.

It wasn't long after we started walking that we ran into Jap troops on the road. They started stripping us of everything we had—watches, rings, wallets, money, cigarettes, etc. Most of us still carried our musette bags with tooth brush, razor, etc., but these were soon emptied onto the road by the Japanese, hoping to find something of value.

Realizing that something like this would probably happen, and money might come in handy down the line, I hid what money I had the night before in my coveralls. I had about $50 in bills, as I recall. To hide it I slit a small opening on the inside of my coverall belt and pushed my money in.

Although the money was well concealed, I was concerned about my compass. I wasn't about to give that up because if escape ever became a possibility, it would be something that I would definitely need. Luckily, there was a perfect place for it in my musette bag.

For anyone that does not know, a musette bag is a small bag made out of very heavy canvass and divided into several compartments where a soldier can carry small personal items such as comb, razor, tooth paste, socks, and underwear.

On the outside there is a small pocket or two where a person could carry something like a pocket watch or a cigarette lighter or something else of similar size.

In the middle of the bag there are five separate compartments, two large and three very small. The large is for socks, underwear and possibly a clean shirt or so, and the small for toothbrushes, comb, and toothpaste. Of the three small compartments the one in the middle was very small. In fact it was so small that a hand could not get in it, but large enough for me to wedge my compass down where it could not be reached or shaken out.

Neither the money or compass were ever found by the Japanese, but the compass did give me causes for serious concern down the line.

As we marched along the road, we soon found ourselves without hats, and something far more critical, water. The Japanese were quick to take our canteens and empty them on the road, and knocked our steel helmets off with their rifle butts.

We were marching through front-line troops that had just overpowered us; they were still inflicting punishment on us in any way that they could.

We endured constant beatings, beatings, beatings every time we ran into a new group down the road. They hit us

American soldiers on Death March out of Bataan

with rifles, sabers, sticks and anything else they could get their hands on. We were half-starved and many so weak they could hardly walk, but they showed us no mercy.

As we walked in no particular order, you could walk as fast as you liked or stall to help conserve energy.

To keep from being beaten by every Jap that came long, I tried to see what was coming up ahead. If the Japanese were beating on the right side, I swung to the left. If they were on the left, I tried to go right. This worked sometimes, but not always. Most places had Jap soldiers on both sides of the road and a beating could not be avoided. Our so-called Japanese guards did nothing to stop this.

When the Japanese emptied my canteen and threw it down, I was able to pick it up again. I knew I would need something for water, but as it turned out I could just as well have left it on the road. Much later during the day, after we had marched in the hot sun without hat or water, some brave soul said that he would try to sneak off the road somewhere and try to get us water. I believe the person was in my outfit, but I don't remember for sure who he was. If I had

Exhausted American prisoner being beaten by Japanese soldier

not known him I am sure I would not have given him my canteen. I also remember that he had more than one. Anyway, to make a long story short I never saw my canteen again.

As it turned out, however, even though some people still had canteens no one was allowed to get water. The day was torture. To begin with we did not know where we were going, and we kept thinking surely it couldn't be much farther, but it was. Much, much farther.

The sun on our bare heads was bad, but the worst was passing up water after water, but not allowed any. After marching well into the dark that day we finally stopped, completely beat and exhausted. We felt surely we would now be given food and water, but that was not to be. They put us in a fenced-off yard and told us through an interpreter that if anyone was found with a knife, razor blade or anything that could be used as a weapon, he would immediately be shot. I thought to myself, They did not say compass, but I knew that I would be in big trouble if they found it.

This place was extremely dark, but there was enough light to see Japanese soldiers with machine guns surrounding us. We were packed like sardines with barely enough room to stretch out and no latrine facilities. If you had to relieve yourself, you did it where you were. I had now gone 48 hours without food and what liquid I had before starting the march was long gone by way of sweat.

There was a lot of talking and moaning going on, but it stopped immediately when we were told we would be shot if they heard any noises out of us again. Needless to say, things quieted down, and that is the last thing that I remember that day.

Next day we were started on the road again before dawn without food or water. Same treatment by the troops heading into Bataan, beatings and more beatings. We were now plodding along like zombies. All we could now think about was water.

The countryside that we were now crossing was a total wreck. The forest was literally destroyed. It looked like a forest fire had gone through it, and all that was left was the skeletons of what was formally giant trees. No remnants remained of what were once villages. The roadside was littered with burned-out trucks and cars, and an occasional tank could be seen. It looked like the total destruction that it was.

The worst part, however, was the dead bodies scattered all over. You could tell that they had been there for some time because they were now all black and bloated. The stench was horrible, and the sight was made more terrible by the swarm of flies around each body.

As we marched along I managed to get a hat off a dead Filipino without the Jap guards seeing me. I assumed he was a Filipino because it was the kind of hat that they wore. It

Dead American prisoner on Death March

was similar in a way to our pith helmets, but made out of coconut fiber. It felt so good to have something on my head. As long as it was not a steel helmet the Japs would let you have it. I think the steel helmets meant front-line troops to them, and they still wanted us to feel totally defeated. We lost a lot of people in the battle of Bataan and so did they. Now they were getting their revenge.

Again, all day long we staggered along that hot, dusty road and though we passed running artesian wells from time to time, we were not allowed to drink. We had long ago stopped thinking about food-now it was water, water. You kept thinking, Where are they taking us? when will it end?

You are thinking, Surely they know that we are exhausted to the point of death, and they would soon relent. But they did not, and we had to muster every bit of strength that we had to carry on.

Many of the sick and wounded had fallen out before now, and the world knows how they were executed as they fell. I saw some of this, but not nearly as much as the people bringing up the rear. I was fortunate in being near the front of the line and had the strength and fortitude to stay on my feet. I was also lucky in other respects, which I will cover later.

As we marched along, the Japanese from time to time would pull out some men for some reason or other. At the time I did not know why, but after the war found out it was to dig trenches and help set up gun positions for their attack on Corregidor. Many of these men were never seen again. Some, I heard later were killed by shells fired from Corregidor. Prisoners of war are supposed to be removed from areas of battle, but true to Japanese behavior, many prisoners never were and died because of it.

All day we looked forward to the end of the heat and misery thinking that at nightfall we would stop like we did the night before. But this was not to be. Darkness came and we kept going.

I decided I was going to get some rest regardless of the consequences. I made up my mind that I would sneak out of the ranks at the next group of trees that we came to. It was very dark, and we were guarded by armed Japanese spaced about 100 yards or so apart. It wasn't long before I spotted some trees up ahead so I moved to the left so that I could make my move. When the time came to go, I took off and landed in some tall grass on the side of the road. I held my breath for a moment, because I wasn't sure if the Jap guards had seen me or not. Pretty soon another guard walked by, and I knew I had made it.

I crawled away from the road and discovered a small nipa hut that was still intact. Apparently a Filipino family had lived here at one time, but now everything had been destroyed except the small outside hut. It still had a door on it. I cautiously crept in and immediately stretched out on the ground.

It was then that I discovered that I was not the only one in the hut. It was occupied by another American soldier as well. He was there for the same reason that I was: rest. We dared not sleep, because if we had, we would have probably slept for hours. Even though it was almost impossible to stay awake, we did.

We could still hear shuffling feet on the road, and we knew we would have to get back in line before long. Before leaving the hut, we noticed that the place contained many empty bottles, either beer or wine. And since neither one of us had canteens, we each took a bottle just in case the Japs decided to let us have water eventually.

I figured that we stayed in the shack about an hour or less before we sneaked back into the line. Again, we were lucky that we were not spotted, but at the time I did not worry too much about it.

Now we had to get water for our bottles, and I made up my mind that at the next water we came to I was going to get some. Sometime later we came to an area where there was a large concentration of Japanese troops, many of whom were bathing and washing around an artesian well.

It was very dark, but I had already made up my mind that some of the next water we would come to would be mine. Not really caring what happened to me, I again slipped out of line and cautiously walked over to the running water. There were Japanese all around me, but luckily no one right at the water, when I got there. I held my bottle under the water for a moment and took off in a low stoop. The water on my hand felt so cool and good and I wanted to stick my head in it and drink, but I knew better. I knew if I got back in line without incident, I had some water. That did happen, and I drank for the first time, since the Japs emptied my canteen two days before.

I did not drink all of the water in my bottle but decided

instead to save some for later, which turned out to be a mistake. Early next morning I had to let my bottle slip through my pant leg and down to the road in order not to be caught with it.

The person, who picked up a bottle with me during the night had also found water somewhere, but the Japanese caught him with it. He was about eight or ten steps ahead of me when they did, and what happened was not pretty. They beat him over the head with the bottle until it broke and kept on beating him with the broken glass. I don't know if he survived or not.

Much as I hated to let my bottle go, I knew then that I had to. I was carrying my bottle under my clothes at the belt line so it was easy to dispose of without being seen. I believe the other person was actually taking a drink when he was caught.

American prisoner being beaten with wine bottle

Long before now we had dumped any excess baggage that we were carrying. A lot of people started the march with blankets, mosquito nets, etc. but by the end of the first day this had all been discarded. It was hard enough carrying your own weight much less anything additional.

For the most part now we were plodding along with strangers. When we found out we were surrendering, the squadron broke up, and we were lucky if we ran into a buddy occasionally. Being together as a unit under such a trying situation would have probably helped, but that did not happen. For a time while we walked we may have recognized a person from our outfit, but before long we would drift apart again and once more be among unfamiliar faces.

The timing of some of these events may not have occurred exactly as I place them now, but I do think that the following took place shortly before dark of the third day.

I was desperate for water even though I had had some the night before. By now many of the men were rushing every well that we came to even though they were being shot as they did so. There were one or two guards close enough to do the shooting so if ten or twelve men went at once, the chances were six or eight would get back without being hit.

Prisoners being shot as they rush artesian well for much-needed water

I decided I would go for it, but would wait until late evening.

The opportunity finally arrived, and I made a dash for it with about ten or twelve others. Shots were fired, but I got a gulp of water without being hit.

The mud around this well was several inches deep and as I started back for the line, I stepped on something that felt round like a can. It was buried in the mud, but I picked it up anyway. It turned out to be a can of *warm* cooked rice, and it was perfectly clean, because it was tightly wrapped in banana leaves. I took this to almost be a miracle. I assumed it was put there by Filipinos, who hoped some tired, starving American would find it, which did happen. I ate it just as soon as it got dark, and it was still warm.

Later on that night, exactly when I am not sure, the Japs stopped us for a short while in what appeared to be a deserted town. They may have been counting us because it seems, as I recall, that they were releasing us a few at a time to get back on to the road. This time I was with a friend of mine from my outfit. As we started walking, we soon found that we were the only ones around. I don't know if we took the wrong road, or street or what, but here we were all alone.

We kept walking and before long ran into two armed Japanese soldiers. They stopped us, naturally, and proceeded to push us around. I was tired, thirsty, hungry and in no mood for abuse so I started pushing back. My friend pulled me back and to this day claims he saved my life, which very well may be true.

He claims that I was delirious, but wrongly so because I knew exactly what I was doing. Somehow or other we caught up with the rest.

Someone reading this may wonder why a person put up with such torture when escape seemed an easy way out. The reason we did not try to escape was the fact that we knew if we did leave we would eventually starve to death because there was nothing left to eat on the entire Bataan Peninsula. It looked like a moonscape.

Also, malaria and dysentery would get us if the Japs didn't first. Escape was not a good alternative yet. Later on some did try and succeeded. Some tried and failed.

About all I can remember about the next day is that it was when I got hold of a canteen.

They put us in an enclosed area, which appeared to me to be in a small town. There were several buildings around our enclosure. They were not nipa huts but gave the appearance of being more like stucco. I vaguely recall that the area where we were held was also surrounded by a high stucco wall and the wall was covered with a vine similar to ivy.

Word quickly spread that we were finally going to be fed and given water. How that rumor got started I don't know, but it did not happen. After a period of about thirty or forty minutes they started marching us out on the road again. The gate that we went in was an opening between one of the houses and the high vine-covered fence.

As we approached this opening on our way out I noticed an army canteen sitting on a small ledge on the side of the house. My first reaction was that the canteen was a trap. You would grab it, and the Jap guards would shoot you for stealing. I thought to myself, Trap or no trap I am going to grab it, which I did as I went by. It was in easy arm's reach and somewhat concealed by more ivy growing on the side of the house.

Another miracle: it was filled with water, but I dared not drink it then. I had to wait until dark to make sure that a Jap guard did not see me. It is unexpected happenings like this that helped us to survive.

This is about the time that I started pulling out of it. By that I mean I no longer expected to stop just up the road to be fed and given water, but now knew that the Japanese intended to march us until we all finally perished. To this day I still believe this to be true, but I was not going to give them that satisfaction.

This day was just as hard as the rest, but somehow I felt better. Getting out of the war-ravaged area may have had something to do with it also. There was still much damage around, but it was not at all like what was seen on the first day of our march.

The fifth day is pretty much of a blank, as I try to recall, except for two incidents. One: I ran into my best friend; two: we should never have slipped off and gone for water. Although little was said between us I was extremely glad to see him. He was one of the guys in the foxhole at Marivales, where we were nearly killed by that bomb.

I don't remember exactly when we met that day, but do recall vividly what happened late that same evening. As always, we were dying of thirst. It was starting to get fairly dark when we came to a wooded area and with the fading rays of sunset could see the reflection of water underneath the trees. There was a Jap guard next to us, so we hit the ditch and crawled toward the water. Before we ever reached it we were almost overcome by this extremely foul odor of something dead. When we reached the water, we found that it held at least three dead bodies that I could see and possibly more. They were half-decomposed, and we could see that they had been there for some time.

Even though I was dying of thirst, I knew this was not for me.

Unfortunately, my friend looked at me and by his expression implied, "What the heck?"

Prisoner drinking out of polluted mud hole

He began to drink, which I am positive caused his untimely death. In about four weeks, he died of dysentery, which I feel sure came from drinking that polluted water. I was gone on a work detail and was not with him when he died but found out about it later when I returned. I sure did miss him and felt alone for a long time afterward.

The next day we reached the town of San Fernando, where we finally stopped, at least for the rest of that day and for that night. Here we were finally fed about a cup full of boiled rice and allowed to have water.

Since I had nothing to put my rice in, I picked up what looked like a wooden shingle and used it for a plate. My fingers were my fork.

This was a hot, dry, dirty place, but as I remember there were a few trees in this yard where we could find some shade. Again, no latrine facilities, which quickly brought the flies to go along with the stench. For the time being this did not seem all that bad, because we now had the most important thing of all—water. The small amount of food was secondary.

At this point many would have said that rest was more important, or appreciated, than the food, because many were suffering from incredibly blistered and bloody feet. My feet were badly blistered, but not as bad as some, who had put on new shoes when they were told to pack up and get ready to break camp. I had no new shoes, otherwise I would have done the same. There is no way for a person to walk as far as we did without getting blistered feet.

We spent the night at San Fernando and next day took off again. No breakfast, of course, but now at least I had a canteen full of water.

By this time we were in an area where the Filipinos had returned to their barrios and nipa huts bordering the road. Damage to property and terrain was not as bad as it was farther to the south, where more fighting had taken place. There were Filipino men, women and children watching us as we wearily walked along.

In several places the women tried to hand food to us, but

the Japanese guards would not allow it. They had bananas, mangos, and coconuts, and it all looked so good. I never saw it happen, but supposedly several Filipinos lost their lives to Japanese bullets when they tried passing food to the Americans. This was the beginning of the end of the march out of Bataan, but we did not know it until sometime that afternoon when we arrived at Camp O'Donnell.

Later on, instead of walking from San Fernando to Camp O'Donnell, the prisoners were moved by train. You would think that this would be a big improvement over walking for the weary men, but it was not. They were stuffed like sardines in box cars and left for hours in the hot sun with the doors closed. Many died from suffocation before they reached O'Donnell. I guess I was lucky that I got to walk, if you can call that luck.

★ 6 ★

Camp O'Donnell

Camp O'Donnell was a training camp for the Philippine Army and was built just prior to the war. It consisted of a series of barracks built in typical Philippine style. The thatched roofs had bamboo frame sides and floors and openings for windows but no screens or shutters. Each barracks was about fifty feet long and could be called a double-decker, because the attic was floored as well.

This attic space may have been for storing personal gear instead of an area for sleeping. I say this, because the highest point between the floor and ceiling, or roof, was only about five feet. It would be cramped even for a short Filipino. I should know because that is where I slept.

Prisoners were apparently being sent out of San Fernando by groups because when we arrived at Camp O'Donnell, I estimated that I was with about two hundred others.

Once we passed through the gate we were made to sit down in an open field, where the law was laid down by the Japanese Commander. I did not pay much attention to what he said except to hear him say that if you did this, you would be shot; if you did that, you would be shot. I wondered what we could do without being shot.

After he was through an American officer walked up and introduced himself as General King. He said that he was the general in charge of the troops on Bataan, and he was solely responsible for our surrender. He told us not to feel bad or discouraged or guilty, because we had nothing to do with it. It was his decision, and if any blame was to eventually come it was his to face.

I had never heard of the general before, but he struck me as a brave and sincere officer. I later learned that he surrendered the troops on Bataan, without orders from Generals Wainright and McArthur, when he realized that to continue fighting was useless considering the condition of the men under his command.

He thought for sure that he would be court-martialed when the war was over because his last orders from McArthur were to attack the enemy, an order which he chose to ignore. He knew that it meant sending hundreds more to their deaths, something that he would not do. Needless to say, he was not court-martialed at the end of the war because everyone by then realized that he did the right thing.

We were finally taken to a barracks, and I decided the best place was up in the loft. I figured it would be the quietest and the least disturbed. I took my only possession from around my neck, my musette bag, placed it on the floor and got some long-deserved rest. The day was about over. Mosquitoes swarmed around my head before I fell asleep, but I did not have the energy to brush them off.

There was no particular order in how we were placed in barracks. That is, units were not reassembled but left scattered. It was probably impossible to do, anyway, because people were still coming in. The only segregation was between officers and enlisted men and Americans and Filipinos. The Filipinos were fenced off in a separate compound. There were about fifty people to a barracks and in my barracks about eight or ten from my outfit.

The next day we were fed about a cup of dry rice again. I was used to eating rice and had no problem with it, but others who had not been around it so much had difficulties with it.

It was cooked in big iron pots similar to the big iron pots that were used in South Louisiana to wash in. We had them at home on the farm, but these were about twice the size. They were so large that the rice on the outside of the pot would burn before the inside got warm.

When I heard that rice was being served, I started searching

for a plate and wound up using a short section of bamboo
that had been split in two. It still had partitions on either
side so it was like a long shallow bowl.

The bamboo was not growing in the prison camp, but was
part of a scrap pile left from the building construction. The
only thing growing in the compound was some small trees
that resembled Chinese tallow. They were no higher than
about six or eight feet and sparsely leafed.

We were now being fed a meager amount of rice, but the
water situation was still critical. There was one very slow-run-
ning faucet out in the yard with a flow capacity of about a
quart every fifteen minutes or so. The faucet was wide open,
and that is all it would deliver. So even now, if and when we
got water, it had to be stringently conserved. There was a
line at the faucet always. Twenty four hours a day. Barely
enough water to drink and definitely not enough to try to
wash with.

It had now been about a week since we broke camp on
Bataan, and we had not been able to wash since. You will be
horrified when I get around to telling you how long I went
without washing.

From here on I won't be able to recount what happened

Only a trickle of water for an endless line of thirsty men

on a day to day basis, but will try to tell what was going on and under what conditions. As I mentioned earlier we were now getting a small amount of rice each day and for a change in menu started getting vegetables. Not the part that you normally eat, but the part that is normally discarded.

We were first given boiled carrot tops. I presume the Japanese were eating the carrots, and they generously gave us the tops. They may as well have kept them because they were inedible. They would not stay down. They were so horrible and strong we would upchuck after a few swallows. When that did not work they tried sweet potato vines, which were terrible but at least they stayed in place. I suspect the Japanese did not want to give us their rice and were looking for a substitute, but could not find one. Eventually we went back to pure boiled, *burned* rice.

By now there were many sick people around with dysentery, malaria, and diptheria. Every conceivable disease was surfacing because of the physical condition of the men and the unhealthy conditions under which they were living. The sick were in such bad shape that they no longer stayed in the barracks, but remained on the outside, some under the buildings to stay out of the sun and some lying outside on the ground near the slit trenches.

Their clothes were all covered with excrement and some had discarded their clothes preferring to be naked. These men had dysentery and to die of dysentery was the most horrible way to go. They had to stay outside or near the latrines because with dysentery you pass blood and mucous every twenty minutes or so. There is no way to keep from it.

I know these men would have preferred dying fighting, instead of in the horrible way that they were now going. Dysentery almost invariably meant death.

How anyone survived I will never know, but something happened shortly after I arrived at Camp O'Donnell which undoubtedly had a lot to do with it.

I think I mentioned that my best friend had drunk polluted water and had come down with dysentery. Well, I now had the initial symptoms even though I did not drink. I was lucky, if you want to call catching dysentery lucky, in that my symptoms occurred a week or so after we reached O'Donnell. I was lucky because I found out that the leaves from the trees found on the prison grounds were a cure for dysentery. I was also lucky because there were still leaves to be found, and I was able to get a good pocket full of them, which I immediately consumed.

In a few days my symptoms disappeared, and, also in a few days, the trees were stripped bare. Apparently word had gotten around that the leaves were a medicine, but there were not enough to go around.

Dysentery spread so rapidly because of the open latrines and the millions of flies around them. They were the same big green flies that we saw on the dead bodies as we walked out of Bataan. There were so many that the branches of the

Hordes of large green flies at Camp O'Donnell

small trees around were bent to the ground. They resembled weeping willows except these could be called weeping-fly trees.

The flies were also hanging by the thousands on the edges of the thatched roofs, because the trees could hold no more.

Sick men were also covered, especially those near the latrine, because the latrine itself held the greatest number. It is no wonder, under these conditions, that so many of the prisoners died.

We had no way to wash and sterilize our so-called plates. I kept mine in the sun hoping that the heat might kill some of the germs. While you were eating, it was a constant fight to keep the flies off your rice. A constant waving of a hand over your food was the only way it could be done and even at that some did manage to slip through.

Besides the flies the stench was something else that was always with us. It was everywhere—inside, outside, on you and everyone else. There was no way to get away from it. It came with the dysentery and by now dysentery was also causing the death of many, many prisoners. They were dying by the hundreds. We heard that as many as 400 were dying each day, and I remember I looked around and tried to determine how many of us were still alive.

I estimated that at the rate we were dying we would all be gone within a month or so. It reached a point where there were so many sick it was decided to put them in a separate section. It was called a hospital (officially), but the prisoners called it the Zero Ward. When you went there that was the beginning of the end. Most died within days. Even though a person was so bad off that he could no longer take care of himself he wanted no part of the so-called hospital. Each day a detail went through the camp picking up the dead and also collecting those considered ready for the hospital.

There was also a daily detail for digging graves, one that I was on regularly. The dead were buried in mass graves with about fifteen to twenty bodies in each. Each grave was about five or six feet wide, eight or ten feet long and about six or

Burial detail at Camp O'Donnell

seven feet deep. About as soon as a grave was finished there were bodies ready to fill it. Every morning a detail was sent to the hospital to collect the dead and then take them to the graves for burial.

I was on this detail several times and it was gruesome. The dead that we picked up were all naked and were nothing but skin and bones. Several of the dead were from my squadron, and one I could only recognize from his teeth.

Each body was carried by four men, although now they weighed practically nothing. The dead were carried on wicker racks, which at one time were probably used as a door or as a window shutter.

When we reached the graves, we just dumped them in the open holes. You could hear the bones crack as bodies were dumped on bodies. This seemed like a terrible way to treat our dead buddies, but since they had all died of dysentery, it was wise to handle the bodies as little as possible. When the hole was full, it was then covered with dirt, but no prayer or religious service was given. Across the road from us the Filipinos were doing the same as we were—burying their dead by the hundreds. They were dying faster than we were, which is something I could not understand.

One day while helping dig graves, I became very sick. It was extremely hot down in the hole where we were, and I started getting dizzy and felt like I was going to faint. I decided to crawl out and find a place to lie down. There was a Japanese guard with us, and I decided I would see if he would let me rest. I started walking toward him, but before I got there my sight left me, and I was completely blind. I decided to collapse, where I was, because I did not want the guard to think that a crazed person was coming after him.

I was burning up with fever and, fortunately, someone took me back to the barracks where I crawled back into my loft. Before long I started having chills, then chills and fever, chills and fever. I finally fell asleep and the next morning when I woke up I could see again. I think I had a heat stroke.

Another scary moment was when I ate some rice given to me by a person who was getting sick. He slept next to me up in the loft. I ate the rice out of his dish because I knew he did not have dysentery. What he came down with two or three days later was diptheria; within a week or so he was dead.

I don't know if it was my imagination or not, but shortly

Grave-digging detail at Camp O'Donnell

thereafter my throat got extremely sore, and I was sure I was coming down with diptheria also. It starts with a sore throat and eventually chokes you to death. A person's throat also is covered with white spots. Anyway, my aching throat finally subsided and I figured I was exposed, but the shots that I had taken when we left the States gave me immunity. Diptheria was a big killer, as was cerebral malaria and beri beri in the early part of our confinement.

There were two kinds of beri beri, the wet and the dry. With the wet, a person's hands and feet swelled enormously, and if the swelling progressed up the legs and into the abdomen, death resulted.

With the dry form there was no swelling, but it brought excruciating pain to the feet and hands with no let up. As far as I know, this type is not fatal. I came down with the wet type, and it did not leave me until I left the Philippines some time later and got off the rice diet.

Another killer was hepatitis or yellow jaundice. I caught it at Cabanatuan Prison Camp, and I still had remnants of it when I got back to the States. Next to dysentery, hepatitis was probably the number two killer in the prison camps. It caused you to lose your appetite, which is one thing you could not afford to do, because the food that you were getting was barely enough to keep you alive as it was. I know I gave up eating entirely for a while.

A friend of mine also came down with hepatitis about the same time as me, but was lucky enough to cure it.

It was a well-established fact there that with a little sugar it could be cured, but sugar was hard to come by. The only way was through the black market and very few prisoners had this opportunity. A few people were on a detail to bring water from a nearby creek back to the camp for cooking. Even though they were guarded the whole time they could, once in a while, get stuff from the Filipinos. One of the things that they were getting was a candy made of coconut and molasses. Since I still had my money in the belt of my clothes, I decided this might be a good place to spend it. I was not able to get my hands on granulated sugar for my hepatitis and thought perhaps the sweet coconut candy would do the trick.

Anyway, I gave my money to a friend, and he was finally able to get some of the candy for us. The candy was wrapped in banana leaves as most things are in the Philippines. For some reason or other we were not able to eat it as soon as we got it, but placed it around my bed for later consumption.

Would you believe it, when we went for it that night it was gone? Two or three days later I left the Philippines for Manchuria, but found out later that the thief was discovered, we did not know it at the time, but he did us a favor by eating our candy. For some reason or other, all those that got hold of this candy came down with dysentery, including the thief, and his stealing caused his death.

Occasionally I refer to my bed or bunk or whatever, but these words are actually misused for what we actually had. Instead of a bed we slept on the bamboo-slat floors without benefit of mattress or blanket. All we had for a cover was the filthy clothes that we had on our bodies. I guess I was lucky because I had my musette bag, which I used as a pillow. I always squeezed it to make sure that my compass was still there. I mentioned earlier that no one was buried with their clothes. They were removed and passed out to the living. I never got any and would not have taken them if they had been offered.

Up to now no one had escaped, but one night it happened. It should not be called escape because these prisoners were caught trying to get back in the prison camp. There were three of them, and they had been out looking for food or medicine. I remember they were put in a cage, near the gate, where prisoners going and coming to and from work details could see them.

The cages were in the hot sun, and they were not given food or water. You could tell that they were suffering miserably, but their suffering only lasted a day or two as I recall because late one evening we were all called out to witness their execution. They were made to dig their own graves and fell into them when shot. Executions like this happened in many of the camps.

After these men were shot the Japanese came up with an idea that they thought would stop prisoners from trying to escape. They put us in what was called "blood brother" groups, and if any one of the group escaped or tried to escape, the rest would be shot regardless of their complicity. Later escapes did cause the death of innocent people.

I never did find out what group I was in, and I always had doubts that they actually had a list of certain people as they claimed. I think what happened when some one escaped was they just collected anyone at hand and executed him. I understand that in one camp one of the prisoners saw his brother shot as a blood brother of some escapees.

About six or eight weeks after we were captured a rumor started floating around about something that was going to happen on the Fourth of July. What was going to happen, no one knew for sure, but several ideas were kicked around. Since the rumor apparently started with the Filipinos, some thought that they would attack the prison camp and set us free.

Others believed it meant that the United States Forces

American prisoners being executed for attempted escape

were on their way and would rescue us by the Fourth of July. This was a rumor that lilted spirits, but just like the help that was on its way to Bataan, it never happened. After the day came and went, many of the men again felt abandoned and decided that such an existence as ours was not worth the price of survival, so they just gave up. Dying was much easier than the fight to stay alive, and many chose this way out.

★ 7 ★

Bridge Detail

One day, while still at Camp O'Donnell, I was selected to go on a work detail away from the camp. I don't know how we were selected or by whom, but I was glad to be getting away from the filth and misery of O'Donnell. I was one of a group of about two hundred that walked out of the prison gates and boarded several Japanese army trucks.

I thought this looks good so far. No long walks. We drove for quite a while and finally came to a small town by the name of Gapan. Here we were housed in what was once a one-room schoolhouse. There was nothing in the school house but a bare wooden floor, which turned out to be our bed.

I picked out a spot and marked it with my musette bag, which I still guarded religiously. Guarded for two reasons: One, it, of course, contained my compass, which I did not want to lose in case an escape became possible, and, second, I surely did not want the Japanese to find that compass because if they did I knew exactly what would happen to me. At O'Donnell my bunk was up in the loft, where I figured searching Japanese would not venture, but here there was no such place. My bag lay on the open floor, and it made me uneasy.

Next morning we were fed a soup of some kind as, I recall, and taken to our work detail.

The work a short distance from our school and turned out to be the rebuilding of an enormous bridge that had been destroyed during the war. The bridge had been over a good sized river. The original was iron and steel, but

Overworked bridge detail at Gapan

was now being replaced by wood. All the metal had already been removed by Japanese workers, and now they were in the process of cutting huge timbers for the frame work.

All of the cutting was done by hand, but not by us. We were given the job of carrying these huge timbers, many of which weighed thousands of pounds, and placing them in their proper positions. Some of these pieces were thirty to forty feet long and about two feet square. It took as many men as could get around them to lift them and even then it was a struggle. In our weakened state I don't know how we did it, but we did.

When we were not carrying and placing timber, we were made to carry rocks from the riverbed up to bridge level, a climb of probably thirty or forty feet, but it felt like scaling Mt. Everest.

We were provided with baskets like the Chinese coolies use: a straight stick that rested on your shoulder with two wicker baskets tied to each end.

There were Japanese guards and others to make sure that each basket had a full load and no skimping took place. A load was very, very heavy and it made for a long day—down to the river, loading up and back up to the bridge. This continued from early morning to about sunset each day.

The only consolation was the food that we were now getting

was better in my judgment. Instead of dry rice we now had a soup of some kind made with vegetables. It was still 90 percent water, and tasted good for a change, but a long way from being enough.

We also had here what could be called our first medicine. We were allowed to make a tea out of mango leaves, which was supposedly good for malaria. I don't know if it helped or not. It certainly tasted bad enough to be good for something.

Apparently the Japanese selected people for this detail who were not obviously sick, but that situation did not last very long. The killing disease that we thought we had left at O'Donnell was now with us at Gapan. Dysentery soon weakened our workforce, and before long prisoners were again dying like flies. This time, however, they were given a more humane burial. They were buried in the local cemetery and placed in individual graves.

Out of all the people that died there was one that I specially hated to see go. He was not a medic, as far as I know, but took it upon himself to help the sick and dying. Some thought he was doing it to have the extra food that the sick would not, or could not, eat. Regardless of his motives he provided help and assistance to the dying and being so close to the horribly diseased he soon became one of them.

When our numbers finally dwindled to about thirty or thirty-five we were finally taken back to the prison camp. We left from Camp O'Donnell, but were taken now to a different camp called Cabanatuan. On the ride back I could not help but notice one guy's foot. It looked like it was rotting away, and I am sure he had gangrene. What impressed me about him was his attitude about his affliction. He seemed even jovial as we rode back to camp. I never saw him again, but it was a miracle if he survived. According to a book written by one of the guys on this bridge detail, only seven of us were still alive at war's end. The person that wrote the book was from my outfit, but I did not know him at the time.

Writing about the prisoner with the bad foot reminded

me of another man who had something terribly wrong with him. I was never sure what his problem was exactly, but it involved his stomach, and I don't know if it was a war wound or what. He wore a very wide rubber band around his stomach, and I was told it was to keep his intestines in. The rubber band was cut from a large inner tube that he slipped into. I never did see his stomach beneath the rubber bandage, but I did see a Japanese guard make him show it to him, and the guard stepped back horrified. I doubt if this prisoner survived.

★ 8 ★

Cabanatuan

Cabanatuan Prison Camp was just like O'Donnell, and it is hard for me to separate them in my mind. It had the same type of buildings. Bamboo frames and floors with thatched roofs. Here, as I recall, I slept on the lower level. It was also here that I caught hepatitis. If I had had it prior to this I would never have gone on bridge detail.

I have trouble separating the two prison camps because one was just as bad as the other. Little water and dirty, filthy living conditions. Back to rice, but now more soupy instead of dry. People were still dying with dysentery and other diseases. I was still in my dirty clothes, clothes that had not been off my body since leaving our camp on Bataan.

The one difference between the two camps was the obvious difference between the Americans captured on Bataan and those captured on Corregidor. Cabanatuan now held prisoners from both places. Prisoners from Corregidor were in much better shape than those captured on Bataan, because they never had the long march to make and they were in better condition when captured. During the war they ate much better than we did so consequently were healthier when captured.

I am not saying that they did not go through Hell, because they did. I am only saying that the Bataan group had it a bit worse. Another thing worth mentioning is that by now prisoners were getting used to the deplorable living conditions to which they were subjected and even to the pall of death that surrounded them. I thought to myself, It would be so nice to die in a clean bed.

Burial detail at Cabanatuan

I did not know the exact month, but some time later we were told we were going to Japan. Again, I do not know how we were selected because some of us left Cabanatuan and some stayed. When I was told that I was going it did not take long to pack, because my complete wardrobe consisted of my musette bag (compass included), canteen and bamboo dish. Oh, yes, I almost forgot my coconut fiber hat.

I remember marching a long distance before coming to a town, where we were then placed in boxcars for our trip to Manila. The boxcars were terribly crowded, but I recall it was better riding than walking.

When we were told that we were going to Japan, the Japanese made it sound like we were going to Heaven. We would be leaving the stifling tropical heat and going to a climate that was cool and comfortable. There we would receive good, plentiful food and excellent housing. When we got there we were promised new clothes, shoes, and soap. They made it sound so good that we were anxious to get going.

Upon arriving at Manila we were again made to march from the train to the docks, where we were to board a ship for Japan. As we walked down the streets of Manila, I remember people staring at us the entire way. They were on both sides of us and were mostly Filipinos and a few

Japanese. As I remember, it was getting dark when we arrived at the docks and instead of putting us aboard a ship, they locked us up in a large warehouse.

As usual we were not fed, but I managed to find something to eat. In one corner of the warehouse there were several sacks of something that smelled to high Heaven. The sacks were the typical Japanese rice straw variety. Even though they smelled, I decided to investigate and found, by the smell, that they contained fish. I now became curious, because fish meant food so I wiggled my hand through the top of the sack and came out with a handful of the stuff. It was fish all right, dried and salted, but not quite what I expected or hoped for. Instead of individual fish of, say, hand size it turned out to be more like dried minnows. Mostly heads, bones, fins and scales, but no noticeable flesh. I decided to sample it anyway, and to my amazement it tasted delicious. Reminded me of the dried fish that my father used to keep in his desk at home for snacks. I don't know how the fish was cured, but the heads, bones, scales, etc. were all soft and edible. What I liked best however, was the salt. It tasted heavenly. I am not positive, but the food that we were getting in prison camps must not have contained salt, but if it did it could not have been very much.

I ate a good handful of the fish and could have eaten more, but was somewhat afraid of what it might do to me. I wasn't sure if the stuff was for human consumption or for something else, but I was not going to walk away from it completely. I figured I ate enough to know how it would affect me or my stomach and if nothing dire happened I wanted more. So, to insure that I would have more, I filled both of my front pockets with the stuff. You can imagine how I smelled now. The odor of a body and clothes that had not been washed in months combined with the powerful smell of dead fish. I was afraid that the smell would give me away when we boarded ship the next day, but it did not.

★ 9 ★

The Ship

The ship that we got on was very large and apparently carried Japanese troops from place to place. I noticed that what appeared to be large guns on deck were actually fakes. They were wooden and the so-called barrels of the guns were made out of the trunks of trees. I also noticed what I took to be depth charges and assumed these to be dummies as well.

I am not sure how many prisoners boarded this ship, but the number was very high. A later estimation put the number at around two thousand.

We walked up the gang plank and were directed to an opening on the main deck. The opening was the forward part of the ship and took us by way of a vertical metal ladder down into a large chamber or "hole" as the Navy would say. The sides of the hole were lined with double-deck wooden stalls, which indicated to me that this vessel was probably used as a troop transport. The stalls were of typical Japanese arrangement. The lower part was about six inches off the floor and the upper stall probably five feet or so above the lower. Unlike those found in the Filipino camps, these bunks were made of solid wood instead of split bamboo.

As prisoners were directed down into the hole, one at a time, it was only natural that they started selecting places on the bunks to claim for their own. Naturally, by the time I got down all the bunk space was filled, but I wasn't concerned. I could stretch out on the steel floor, which I felt would be cooler than the wooden stalls. We found out that no one was going to stretch out, and it turned out the so-called bunk space was worse than the floor.

I still can't help but chuckle when I remember some one calling up to the Japs that the place was full after all the stalls were taken. Little did he know that the place was not even half full considering the number that was eventually packed in. We would end up like sardines, except we were packed vertically instead of horizontally.

It turned out that I was lucky to be on the floor, because even though I could not lie down and stretch out, I could at least sit and stand. People crowded in the sleeping bays also did not have room to stretch out, but they also did not have enough head space to stand up.

By now the ship was getting unbearably hot from the heat of the tropical sun and the large number of prisoners in such a confined space added to it. It was quickly turning into agony, but we had not seen the worst.

Because many of the prisoners were still coming down with dysentery, toilet facilities soon became a problem. All we had was a bucket on top side, and the Japanese guards would only let about two people out at a time. It wasn't long before people were crowded at the ladder wanting to use the so-called facility. And it also wasn't long before the place became a stinking cesspool. It began to look again like Camp O'Donnell.

People soiled their clothes and everyone and everything around them. If anything, it was worse than O'Donnell because now everyone was confined in a small, overcrowded space, and you could not get away from it. Getting drinking water was also just as bad because it was also on top side, and you got it when you went to the latrine. Luckily food was sent down in a wooden bucket. It was the same old soupy rice.

About the third day out of Manila we really got a scare. All of a sudden we could feel the ship make a hard right turn, which seemed unusual, and within minutes large explosions began taking place all around us.

The explosions were strong enough to rock our ship, and my first impression as to what was happening was that we were being attacked by American naval ships.

I considered the explosions to be large shells striking the water nearby and even though we were in a hole below deck I was hoping that we would be sunk.

I figured that many of us would be killed or drowned, but I was willing to risk it because I also knew some would survive and be picked up by friendly forces. I was wrong all the way around.

It was friendly forces all right, but instead of a surface ship after us it was a submarine. The sub fired two torpedoes but missed with both. The Jap captain saw them coming and was able to swing the ship around just in time to avoid them. One missed us by about fifty feet, according to a report that we saw later about this attack.

The depth charges that I saw on topside, when we first got on this vessel, were not fakes, but were the real thing. The tremendous explosions that we felt were those depth charges going off as they were rolled off the deck into the water. According to the two prisoners using the facilities at the time, the Japanese panicked and began to immediately drop depth charges overboard even though the sub was probably thousands of feet away.

I think we came closer to being sunk by the Japanese on board ship than the friendly sub off in the distance. According to our guys that saw the whole thing, the torpedos had already surfaced, indicating that they had been shot from a considerable distance.

As they splashed through the surface they became visible to the Jap skipper, giving him time to avoid them. It was exciting while it was going on, but after it was all over we began to wonder if it was actually all over. As far as I know, our ship was alone at the time, and we felt that our attacker would not give up so easily. We had probably used up all or most of our depth charges, and our cannons were fakes.

We were a sitting duck, and we seriously expected to be attacked again at dark that day, and if not then, surely at dawn next morning. There was a lot of sweating going on for the next few days, but nothing again happened.

As expected under such conditions, people began to die. At first it was maybe one or two a day and some days none, but eventually it got up to several every day. Most of the dying occurred at night for some reason, and in the morning they were passed up to the Japanese to be thrown over board. Nights were probably more stressful because the hole that we occupied was in total darkness. You could not see a thing, but could hear the constant moaning of men in agony.

One night all bedlam broke loose. There was loud screaming and thrashing of disturbed bodies, which caused a considerable uproar. In the dark you could tell that many people were involved, even though they could not be seen. Next morning we found out what happened.

One of the prisoners had gone mad and had started attacking everyone around him with his canteen. When he severely hurt several around him, it was obvious that he could not be restrained. He was killed by those around him with his own canteen. Next morning he was lifted out of the hole with several others and slipped overboard. His troubles were over.

After the submarine attack, we joined a Japanese convoy of ships led by several naval vessels. Now that enemy submarines were around, the Japs were not taking any chances. It was not our lives that they were concerned with, but theirs.

We found out later that a ship loaded with prisoners was sunk by a U.S. submarine and most aboard perished, but a few did survive and were rescued by the sub that sank them. This is the kind of situation that I was hoping for when we were shot at.

We must have taken a zig-zag course from then on, because it seemed like our journey would never end. Eventually after about three or four weeks, we came to a complete stop. We could hear voices on the outside as our ship was tied up. We had finally arrived in Japan, so we thought, but that was not yet the case. We soon learned that we were in a Taiwan harbor.

Eventually we were all removed from the ship and placed on an open dock nearby. Word got around that the Japanese were going to clean out the ship, which sounded great Now that we were back out in the open and breathing clean, fresh air it felt like we had risen from the dead. It was very chilly, but it felt good after coming out of that stinking, filthy, hot hole where we were imprisoned for all those days.

I don't know if this was their original intention, but after they saw how dirty and filthy we were they decided also to clean us up as well as the ship. They made us strip completely and then blasted us with water from fire hoses. The force of the water hurt and stung, but it felt good.

We had no soap but that was all right. This was the first water I had on my body since we left our bivouac on Bataan. We were also stomping on our wet clothes hoping to work out some of the dirt and crud there as well as that on our bodies.

While this was going on there was a crowd of Taiwanese onlookers taking all this in. There were both men and women. It was about now that I noticed my own body. I was shocked and horrified by what I saw. It was not the dirty body as such, but the physical condition of that body. I had dwindled to skin and bones and had not been aware of it. My legs and arms were completely devoid of muscle and flesh and I looked like a living skeleton. I was as skinny as the men who had died of dysentery; it really shook me up to discover this. All the while my arms and legs and body were covered with coveralls and I was not aware of what was happening to me. I knew I still had a difficult struggle ahead of me if I wanted to survive and return home someday.

When the hoses were finally turned off, we put back on our still dripping-wet clothes. Apparently it was taking a long time to clean out the ship because we stayed on the dock for some time.

By then we were getting extremely cold and uncomfortable and were anxious to return to the ship. I am not sure what time of the year it was, but my guess is late October or November.

Washed down with fire hoses on pier at Formosa

When we finally did get back on the ship we found our so-called quarters still dripping wet and now very cold. Even after we were all back, it still did not feel warm. By now, because of the number of prisoners that had died, there was a little more space for everyone.

I remember that one guy, who had had a bunk position, now had enough room to lie down. He was even kind enough to give me his space from time to time to stretch out and take a nap.

It's funny, but we never did learn each others' names. I think it was best that way, because if the person died you would not take it so hard. Just another stranger gone.

I remember when we got back on ship an American officer cautioned us about getting pneumonia. He told us to try to dry ourselves and avoid getting chilled which was actually impossible. This was the first American officer that I had seen on board, and he was clean and dry. From that I assumed he was staying in much better quarters than the rest of us, which was true.

About a day or two after we left Taiwan I began to get sick. I was not too concerned about it at first, because it appeared that I was coming down with a cold. What may have started out as a cold soon developed into something much more serious. Before long the right side of my chest began to hurt, and the pain got so bad that I could hardly breathe. I reached a point where I was too sick to eat and could not even go for my food as it was being dished out. I was sick, sick, sick.

Before long my left side began to hurt as well and breathing now became even more painful. All I could tolerate was taking in, and expelling very small amounts of air because of the pain. Finally, after many days, I felt the ship slow and come to a halt again. I thought, Japan at last, and now I might get medical help and medicine for my sickness and pain. We had been at sea a week or more since our last stop at Taiwan.

Before long prisoners were crawling up the ladder and out of the hole until the place was almost empty. With my musette bag around my neck and my canteen in it I made an attempt to cross over to the ladder, but that was not to be. I could not even rise much less walk.

Pretty soon two Japanese soldiers came down into the hole and started lifting the sick and dying to other Japanese above. I was not the only one unable to move. When they came to me they lifted me to my feet and drug me over to the ladder.

They wanted me to crawl up and out, but that was impossible. I was too weak, and I hurt too much. When they saw that I could not do it, each Japanese guard grabbed me by the arms, lifted my arms above my head and handed me to waiting guards above. The Jap guards above grabbed me by my wrists and lifted me out.

How I survived this ordeal I shall never know. The pain that I felt when being lifted by the arms was excruciating. I had never felt anything like it before nor have I felt anything come close since.

Once out of the hole and off the ship, the Japanese placed the sick off to one side of the main group of prisoners. Eventually the main group took off without us. Before long several army trucks drove up, and we were bodily thrown on

Being pulled from the ship's hole at Pusan, Korea

to the back of them. I remember being picked up by my arms and legs and swung and dumped on the truck bed like a sack of potatoes would be handled. This I judge to be the second most painful experience of my life. Second to the pain that I felt when I was lifted out of the hole of the ship.

★ 10 ★

Pusan, Korea

The truck ride that followed was no joyful experience either. Now my bones began to take a beating as I lay on the metal bed of the truck. I was being bounced around because of a very rough road, and I had no flesh on my bones to cushion each bounce. Again pain and misery. When would it end?

Finally we arrived at what appeared to be an army camp, and the trucks drove up to one of the barracks. Once inside we found the place to be very clean and nice and warm. There was snow on the ground outside, which accounted for the heat inside. There were even straw-filled mattresses and blankets for each man.

Even in my sick and weakened condition, I felt buoyed up by what I saw. I thought to myself, Japan is not bad and is a far cry from what we had in the Philippines. We learned a little later that we were not in Japan, but in a place called Pusan, Korea. I had never heard of it before.

I later estimated that there were about fifty or sixty of us brought to this camp, and to this day I am not sure if it was Japanese or Korean. Each day we were visited by a doctor and one or two others with him. Once again I don't know if he was Japanese or Korean.

The doctor could speak a little English and said that I had pneumonia. I was given a small amount of white powder each day, but I don't know what it was. It was folded in what appeared to be a cigarette paper. As in all places I had previously been, people were dying at the rate of two or three a day. They were picked up in the morning when

114

the doctor came in, and taken out and cremated.

Next day or so their ashes would be brought back in an urn and placed on a shelf in the barracks.

By then you could tell when a person was about to die. They had what we called a death grin. The skin was stretched so tightly across their fleshless faces that their mouths stayed permanently open, as though grinning. A person in that condition was not long for this world.

There was another condition that we called the death rattle. This also meant death within a few days. I was shocked beyond belief one morning when the person next to me said that during the night I was making the rattling sound. After that I was afraid to go to sleep, because that was usually when a person died.

I remember fighting to stay awake night after night. The nights seemed to last an eternity and I remember how glad I was to hear the sound of crows in the distance. It meant morning was near and I was still around. You reach a point where dying becomes easy, but staying alive is a battle. Many chose not to fight any longer. The guy on the side of me eventually died of trench mouth, of all things. I knew it killed many soldiers in World War I, but this was the first that I heard about in this war. I was told later that it is easily cured with medicine nowadays, but then it still killed.

Eventually I started feeling better. I was able to breathe more normally without much pain, but I was still very, very weak. I even began to eat more and now the food that we were getting was a lot more nutritious and very tasty. It was a rich vegetable soup with some meat. It was apparently the same food that soldiers in this camp were getting. The food, living accommodations and personnel indicated to me that we were now in the hands of Koreans and not the Japanese. Now we were being treated a little more like humans.

Back then I had no good estimate of time gone by, but I would say that after two or three weeks the dying ceased. There were about twenty or twenty-five of us left, and we were slowly starting to get out of bed and move around some. One day the guards got us all up and took us outside. We thought it was for the fresh air, but it turned out to be for a walk.

This camp was in a pine or evergreen forest, and the terrain was slightly hilly. Our barracks was right on the edge of the forest and a path close by led into the woods. This is the path or trail that we took.

I remember that it was very cold with snow underneath trees in places, but the smell of conifers was invigorating. Before long, however, I wondered if I had made a mistake by coming on this walk. I tired very rapidly and the exertion caused me to breathe deeply, causing my lungs to hurt again. The trail went up and down until I thought I would collapse from fatigue and hurt. Somehow I managed to hold on until we got back, but it was not easy. I don't imagine the walk was more than a quarter of a mile, if that, but it seemed like one hundred. Although it was difficult for all of us, I am sure it did us a world of good.

When we got back we were all given an apple. I ate mine raw and it tasted so good, but one of the men baked his in our stove. Almost every day from now on we were taken outside to exercise. No more hikes but fast walking, and even some slow running. I was still at the slow-walking stage, still very weak and unsteady on my feet.

One day we were told that we were leaving and for everyone to pick up an urn of ashes to take with him. As we walked out of the building, I noticed an old battered pith helmet in the corner so I grabbed it as I went by. My Filipino hat had long since disappeared, and I figured something for my head would probably come in handy somewhere down the line.

Outside we boarded a truck again, but now we were able to sit upright on the bed of the truck, because we were not so sick as we were before.

The road was again bumpy, and it did hurt my boney body a bit, but this time it was easier to take.

Before too long we arrived at a railroad station and were put in a coach. Naturally we had it all to ourselves with our ever-present guards at each end. The curtains were drawn so that we could not see out. Eventually we pulled out, and as I remember it was now dark.

Sometime next day I sneaked a peek to see what was on the outside as we went by. It was a quick glance, but I did get to see a countryside of rolling hills with many small pine trees covering the hills. The trees were in neat rows and had obviously been planted.

I don't remember being fed on this trip, but I did not care. By now I was surely used to going without food for long periods of time.

One thing that I am not sure of in my mind is when the Japanese finally gave us new clothes and shoes to wear. It may have been when we left Pusan or when we arrived at the camp in Manchuria. In any event, it does not make a great deal of difference. As I think about it now, however, I believe we were given gowns to wear in the barracks at Pusan so apparently our filthy clothes were thrown away. If that is right then we were undoubtedly provided with new clothes at Pusan before we left.

The clothes that we were given were all Japanese Army issue: shoes, cap, shirt, pants, socks, underwear, and coat. These were Japanese summer uniforms and clothes and not the woolen uniforms that our guards were now wearing. We were given only one of each item, but at least we now had something that was new and clean.

We hated having to wear a Jap uniform, but we really had no choice. Japanese uniforms were not at all like ours. The soles and heels of the shoes were studded with nails to make them last longer, and the socks had no heels. They were the tube variety, which I had never seen before.

The jacket was similar to most jackets, but the pants or trousers were not. The legs tapered down to the ankles and had tie strings to make them snug against the skin. The belt area was similar except it was made to overlap and wrap around the body and then tied with attached cords. The shirt was collarless and very light. We had no undershirt.

Now we were on a train going somewhere, but no one had the slightest idea where. All we knew was that we were in Korea riding on a train—that was it. I can even remember not being much concerned. Except for not eating, this was the most comfortable situation that I had encountered since the war began.

We knew that we were going to join the rest of the prisoners. After a very long ride the train stopped.

It was late in the evening of the next day. This time we were in a large city, but the train had stopped someplace other than at a depot.

We were made to exit and found ourselves on what appeared to be an open yard associated with a railroad siding. The place looked and felt like the inside of a deep freezer. Everything was covered with snow, and the ground was frozen solid.

Instead of marching us off, or doing something to keep us warm, the guards just kept us standing. In our light clothes it did not take long for us to start freezing. You have to remember that we were skin and bones under those clothes and our bodies could not generate much heat. I don't know how long we were made to stand, but I do know that within minutes my feet became numb up to my ankles from the cold. My whole body was shaking from top to bottom and I could not stop it.

Luckily a truck finally arrived, and we were put in back. I needed help because I was too weak to board; the feet that I could not feel did not offer any assistance.

Before long we were on our way and unlike the warm, comfortable train ride that we just left we were now being buffeted by a stinging, extremely cold wind as we moved along.

The city disappeared in the distance and we kept on going. We went through a very small community, and we kept on going. We finally came to a group of buildings that resembled an army camp with the whole place surrounded by a barbed-wire fence. I knew this had to be our destination, but where were we?

★ 11 ★

Mukden, Manchuria

I remember there were several buildings, possibly a dozen or more, but I am not sure of the exact number. The buildings were low to the ground, and barely visible because of the thick blanket of snow that covered everything. Each building was about fifty feet long, more or less, and about fifteen to eighteen feet wide. They seemed so short. (We soon found out that they were half buried in the ground to keep out the cold. The buildings had no windows as I recall.)

I was happy to see a small column of smoke coming from some of the buildings because that meant warmth, which is something that I was eagerly looking forward to. When we got to the gate the guards looked us over and waved us on through.

We stopped shortly at one of the buildings and unloaded. Again I needed assistance. We were then led to the door of a building and had to step down several steps to enter. This is when I found out that the buildings were half buried.

Once inside, the place felt comfortable. Some of the prisoners who got here before us had built a fire in our stove and were there to greet us. It made me feel very good to see them again, although I did not recognize anyone.

I wasn't in the building more than five minutes when one of the men said that my nose was frozen or frostbitten, and I had better quickly do something about it. I knew if my nose was frozen surely my feet were also.

The guy ran outside to get some snow to rub on my nose while I pulled off my shoes. Sure enough, my feet were much worse than my nose. I rubbed my nose with snow while he did the same to my feet until I finally could feel them again.

Both my nose and feet blistered horribly and turned black and blue like a bad bruise. The skin eventually peeled off, and I was fine except for some badly scarred feet. Before long the guys brought in a bucket of hot soup and it was served in a ceramic bowl with a metal spoon to go with it.

We also found out that we were near the city of Mukden, Manchuria. We had come from the furnace of the tropics to the deep freeze of the Arctic. What a move! I suspect that the temperature on the outside when we arrived was near zero Fahrenheit or, if not that, in or below the teens.

The ceiling in the barracks was about seven feet at its high point with exposed beams of 2 x 4s. There was also one sleeping level about 6 inches from the ground. I say ground because, as I recall, the floor was dirt instead of wood. A very primitive structure. Probably an old Manchurian army base that had been abandoned, but now reopened for our confinement.

Each building probably held about thirty or forty people, and each person was provided with a straw-filled mattress and four blankets in winter. There was one stove to a building, and each stove was provided with one scuttle of coal per day.

Our lights consisted of two hanging light bulbs. We also got to keep the spoon and bowl we received on our arrival. The people who arrived earlier were given heavy overcoats, but we did not get them just yet.

Each person selected a spot, and I was pleased to find a good friend bunking next to me. He was from my outfit; I didn't know until then that he was part of the group that was left in Pusan. He had a very bad case of beriberi and another disease, the name of which I can't recall.

Before long it was lights-out time, and I again became aware of how weak I was. I tried to crawl under my blankets, but could not lift them. Eventually, with the help of others, I managed to make it. The covers felt good for a while, but before long my body began to ache from the weight of the covers, and I had a miserable night. If I removed the blankets, I would freeze, and if I left them on I would hurt. I decided hurting was better, because I was used to that by now.

It was the next day, or close to it, that the Japanese came around and gave each man a number. Mine was 1439. In Japanese it was itchy, yon, son, coo. I am not sure if the spelling is correct, but that is what it sounded like. We had to quickly learn to count in Japanese, because every day we were counted several times by sounding off like the U.S. Army.

About this time we were also weighed. We were placed on a foot scale. I figured I weighed under 90 pounds after subtracting some for shoes and clothing.

The food here was not as good as at Pusan, Korea, but much better than what we received in the Philippines. Here we were served maize (ugh!) soup for breakfast, soy-bean soup for lunch and dinner and a small bun once a day. Breakfast was terrible. It reminded me of a soupy tapioca, but instead of being clear, it was a sickly blue. The soy bean soup tasted good if compared with the maize, and with the sorry stuff that we got at O'Donnell and Cabanatuan.

All of the cooking was done by Americans, and the food was distributed to each barracks in a covered wooden bucket. There was a dipper that came with it, and each person was given one dipper full.

Since all of the beans in bean soup sink to the bottom, no one wanted to be served first. The first served may only have, at best, a dozen beans, while the last person served could wind up with several times that many.

To avoid conflict a rotating system had to be started. If you were first today, you would be last tomorrow. It was a fair system and suited everyone.

The bean soup that we had was very thin with a ratio of something like 90 percent water and 10 percent beans.

If there were any seconds to be served that was also closely monitored. Usually there would be five or six people that got seconds, and since it was the bottom of the bucket, it had the highest bean count of all.

Since rice was scarce in Manchuria, the Japanese kept it for themselves and gave us beans instead. Going to beans from rice, I am sure, saved many prisoner's lives, and I am almost positive it saved mine. Beans are rich in vitamins and protein while rice is a starch or carbohydrate.

I recall one mineral that we got in the Philippines and that was iron. We got it from scraping the rust from old nails that we found lying around on the ground. The powdered rust was then sprinkled on our rice.

Some American Army doctor put out this bit of advice. It was something that you did on your own. I don't know how many prisoners tried it, but I know that I did. I was willing to try anything that might help me survive.

Each morning the prisoners that were well were lined up, counted and marched off to work at a factory on the outskirts of Mukden. Just at dark they would return, be counted and go to their barracks. They were served breakfast just before they left in the morning and supper just as soon as they arrived at night. Shortly after supper lights had to go out, and all had to be in bed. Japanese guards made frequent visits during the night to make sure that everyone was in bed and, more importantly, to make sure that everyone was still there.

It was several months before anyone from my barracks (the Pusan group) became strong enough to work, but gradually it did happen. We slowly gained some weight, and strength returned to our emaciated bodies. The first indication of weight gain came in the face. The face was filled out with puffy cheeks, but the rest of the body was still skin and bones. Next came a protruding stomach. Very odd looking, a fat face, large stomach but skinny, skinny body. Finally the legs and arms began to fill out. No one really got fat, but now they were in much better shape.

Contrary to expectations, coming to a cold climate did

Marching to factory from old camp in Mukden, Manchuria

not stop the dying. The first winter was the worst with the killers still being dysentery and hepatitis, and now pneumonia was added to the list. A building was set aside as a "hospital," but it was very similar to the "Zero Ward" of O'Donnell and Cabanatuan.

Luckily, I was a patient at Pusan and not here in this camp from what I observed. I visited the place just once to see a friend, and I was appalled at what I saw. Men in misery and suffering. Just as it had been where ever we were. After Pusan, I guess I expected this place to be similar, but it was not.

I did not see any Japanese doctors, and, as far as I know, there were none, not then or ever. Here the sick and dying had a new scourge, body lice. They were crawling all over by the thousands, body, hair, clothes—you name it they were there.

In the heat of the tropics it was flies, and here it was body lice. Body lice probably spread germs as readily as flies. Everyone had lice, but those who were well enough were able to keep the number of lice down.

They got in the seams of your clothes when they were not biting you, and that is where you looked for them. As they were discovered they were squashed between the fingernails exposing blood that they had sucked from your body.

The Chinese coolies did not let them get away with their

blood because they ate them when they were discovered. A Chinese coolie at rest was always searching for lice. Come to think of it, we were, too, at least at this time.

During that first winter all the dead were placed in a storage building. That was necessary because the ground was frozen solid, making it impossible to dig graves. Burial could not, therefore, take place until mid- to late spring. When the time arrived, a large burial detail was sent out to dig graves. Even then digging was difficult, because only the top eight to ten inches of the ground was thawed with frozen, rock-hard soil below. This was permafrost country.

When the graves were finally dug, we went for the bodies. We found them stacked like cordwood, because they were still frozen solid. As in the Philippines they were all naked. They looked like skeletons with skin stretched over their bones. The one difference was many of the bodies were lemon yellow. They had died from hepatitis, or so-called yellow jaundice. Although it was prevalent in the tropics, it was catching up with us now.

For some reason or other, my case only made me lose my appetite for awhile and turned my eyes yellow, but fortunately that was it. Since these bodies were yellow, I assumed they died of hepatitis, but in reality it could have been a combination of diseases.

The bodies were carried to the gravesite which was on a small hill located out in the country not too far from our camp. Bodies were placed in individual graves, and when all were buried prayers were offered and some religious songs sung, such as "The Old Rugged Cross" and "I Come to the Garden to Pray." It was very touching and sad and so much better than the burials at O'Don-nell and Cabanatuan.

A large wooden cross was also erected, which seemed appropriate. I don't know how many were buried this date, but the number was large. In the building where they were stored, I remember a stack of bodies over head high and possibly twenty-five to thirty feet wide. Luckily, after this first winter there were fewer deaths.

The winters were unbelievable. Everything was frozen solid. In fact, the ground was frozen so hard that the sound of one's footsteps could be heard penetrating the soil like the ring of a bell.

The sun never came out bright and clear, which made for hazy days. Fog seemed to cover everything. The only indication of a sun was a dim bright spot in a very hazy sky.

I recall a few times when the faint glow of the sun appeared in as many as six to eight different locations in the sky at the same time. These bright spots were all identical and it was impossible to tell which was the real sun. It was all very weird and looked like a place out of this world. I read about these multiple-sun images in a magazine many years later.

The only place that came close to being as cold as this was in Wyoming. I think the coldest there was -45 degrees F. Here we know it got down to -49 degrees F, and possibly even colder at times. Just like in Wyoming, your eyelids froze shut and your clothes frosted up on the outside.

In this camp we still did not have bathing facilities, and, as I remember, we melted snow to get water to wash our hands and faces with. The last water on my entire body was the hosing at Taiwan.

Latrine facilities were on the outside, and a person almost froze before accomplishing his mission. All you could do was pull your pants up, and holding them with your arms, run for cover. Your hands were too numb from the cold to do any tying of strings. There were other parts of your body just as cold, if you know what I mean. Gee, but it was cold.

No one ever expected it to happen here, but it did in the dead of winter. Two men escaped one night by crawling underneath the barbed-wire fences and avoiding the guards. Their disappearance was not discovered until next morning. Apparently they rigged their bunks to look like they were still there, which was sufficient to fool the night guards that inspected the barracks.

No one was sent to work that day, because the Japanese

were trying to find out if any one else was involved. I still could not believe that anyone would go at this time of the year. How did they expect to survive under such extreme conditions outside? You could even see the tracks that they made in the snow. Tracks that led to the fence, where they went under and presumably tracks on the outside. I believe that they made it, because the Japanese guards, possibly Manchurian guards now, were not walking their beat like they should have been, because of the cold.

Luckily the men that escaped were not from my barracks. We were all too weak to try, anyway, so we were no candidates. The prisoners from the escapees' barracks, however, were thoroughly grilled by the Japanese, who were trying to find out if others were involved or if they knew of the men's plans beforehand.

Besides the grilling, their barracks was completely searched, the Japanese looking for what I don't know, but it gave me an uneasy feeling knowing that I had a compass in my belongings. I thought about burying it in the snow, but decided to leave it where it was, I had come this far with it and so far got away with it, so why panic now?

In their investigation the Japanese implicated one other prisoner, rightly or wrongly I don't know, but I do know that he was placed in solitary confinement, where he stayed until war's end. As far as we could tell, when he was finally released, and we got to see him, his mind appeared gone, and I don't know if he knew what was happening.

After a while things quieted down, and we thought that the guys had made good their escape. However, this was not the case. One morning we saw them at the prison gate. Their hands were tied or handcuffed behind their backs, and they looked tired and beaten. They had taken a high risk gamble and lost, and we all felt for them.

Our next concern was would the Japanese now pull out "blood brother" groups and execute them the way they did in the Philippines? Luckily here in Manchuria, they apparently did not know about blood brother justice because no one beyond the one implicated was punished. The two American escapees were eventually taken away and never seen again.

As I recall, the civilian prisons were searched after the war looking for these men, but they were not found.

I should also mention that the Japanese picked up a Chinese person at the factory, where they all worked, who, they claimed, was also involved in the escape. He undoubtedly suffered the same fate as the Americans. It was common practice for the Japanese to parade escapees in front of other prisoners to show them that they could not get away with it. Undoubtedly having our two escapees at the front gate for a while was for that same purpose.

After the men escaped the Japanese started making us guard ourselves. We now had to have our own men guard the doors of the barracks to prevent people from leaving. If someone took off, then the guards would be responsible and suffer the consequences. This was much better than the Philippine system of punishment. In the Philippines it would be the entire blood brother group, ten shot for each man that escaped. Here it would only be the two guards at the doors of the barracks where the men escaped.

★ 12 ★

The Factory

Eventually I was well enough to go to work and was really looking forward to it. My long period of recovery was boring, and I was glad it was over with. One morning after breakfast, I lined up outside with the rest of the men to be counted. Once done we marched out of the gate with accompanying guards. I had no idea how far the factory where we worked was from our camp, but I was told it was a considerable distance.

Well, we walked, and we walked, and we walked. At last we came to a small community of houses, a village of sorts, but that was not it so we kept on going.

After much, much more walking we finally arrived at the factory gate. By now I was bushed. At the gate we were lined up and again counted before entering and, once inside, taken to our assigned building.

The factory was called MKK (I never knew exactly what the letters stood for). The entire place was put up by the Ford Motor Company, which planned to make cars and trucks there. Presumably it was abandoned because of the war since it was never completed. The factory buildings were huge and all alike. Each measured several hundred feet long and about 100 feet wide. On the inside were dozens of huge American machines still in their unopened crates. The floor of the buildings was still dirt. Our job was to cement the floor, make sturdy foundations for the machines, set them up and start production. The Japanese figured American machines run by Americans equaled mass production. Little did they know.

After work that first day we were counted at the factory before we left, made the long march back to camp, where we were counted again at the gate and released to the barracks just at dark. As soon as we got in we were fed and shortly thereafter lights out. I estimate the walk to be at least five miles one way and possibly more. It was a lot of walking.

Next morning it was up, counted, served breakfast, outside, counted, marched to the factory, counted, work and a reversal of everything to get back to camp. This went on day after day, and it soon got monotonous. I forgot to mention that we were thoroughly searched before being allowed back in camp. Sometimes the searching was haphazard, but sometimes it was very thorough even to the point of complete stripping of clothing, which in the winter time was very uncomfortable.

Our lunch was served at the factory. It was the same soy bean soup that we had at camp and the quantity was about the same, which was a cup or thereabouts. I don't remember if we got a bun with our noon meal or not. Irregardless, we were not getting enough to eat anyway and were always hungry. One small bun was not enough extra to help very much.

To pep up our soup at the factory some of the men were able to steal some peanut oil, which when added to the soup made it taste very good for a change. In fact, it was delicious, at least that is what I thought at the time.

When we were in prison camps in the Philippines, our strongest want or desire was water. Food was secondary. Now that we had sufficient water it was food that was constantly on our minds.

I remember how we used to say that if we ever got back to the States we would carry food with us wherever we went. If we had a house it would be full. If we had a car, the trunk would be loaded. The pockets of our clothes would also be stuffed with candy bars and peanuts. We could at least dream if nothing else.

Another thing that was stolen was glycerin, which was added to the breakfast menu to sweeten it. I never had any, and I strongly doubted that sweetening maize would do much to make it more appetizing. It probably would help the mush that we occasionally had. I don't know what the glycerin was used for at the factory, but the peanut oil was a replacement for petroleum as a lubricant. Getting hold of these two products was not widespread, and I only got hold of peanut oil once or twice.

The early or first work that we had to do at the factory was to lay down a cement floor in each building, which was quite a task since it was all done by hand, no mechanical cement mixers. Next, we had to dig out big areas of the floor where, after being filled with concrete, all would become sturdy foundations for the machines. The holes were dug according to a plan laid out by the Japanese. I wondered why we did not finish the foundations first and then pour the floor, but it was not my job to say.

It was hard work tearing up the floor again at each machine location. The machines that were in crates were brand-new and consisted of metal lathes, large drill presses, extremely large shapers and others that I was not familiar with. Most of these required very strong foundations to keep them from cracking the floor and also probably to make them more steady when operating.

Some of the larger foundation holes were about 3 to 4 feet deep, 8 to 10 feet long and about 4 feet wide. Others were about the same depth, but not as long and as wide. The big shapers took the big foundations.

We did not dig all the holes at once but instead would dig out one or two and fill it with concrete and continue this sequence. In the meantime we had discovered that each crated machine had a small wooden box stuck in a corner.

Closer investigation revealed that the wooden box contained handles, knobs, dials, screws, bolts, etc. In other words, precision tools and essential parts that went with the machine. Right away we knew what we had to do with them. Get rid of them.

We first started this by taking the smaller parts and dumping them in the latrine; it was the same old saddle-trench style, but eventually got bolder. When a hole was completed and ready to be filled with concrete, some one would grab a bunch of parts and throw them in the hole, where they were quickly covered. Without these important parts, the machines would be useless.

In one instance I know of an entire metal lathe was buried this way. You may be wondering, Where were the guards? There were always one or two guards around, but they could not constantly watch what every man was doing. Also with all of the large, crated machines around sabotage was relatively easy.

After most of the machines were in place, and the Japanese found that they were inoperable because of missing parts, they put us to work making various small tools by hand, such tools as pliers, snips, and dividers. I was in a group making metal dividers.

Each group contained about twenty men and all had Japanese civilian instructors or advisors. Every man was given a vice and a file and put to work. Before long I was made an instructor with another guy, and all we had to do was check other people's work.

The Japanese instructor that we had was fairly old, and I think he quickly became discouraged with our progress so he handed the responsibility to his instructors.

I was happy, and the only thing wrong with it was that it made the days long. With all of the effort expended we never had a pair good enough to send out. A good pair of calipers should have perfectly straight sides and when riveted together the two sides should touch at the tips when closed. On our calipers this never happened. The only way to get the ends to meet or touch on our calipers was to bend and twist the sides a bit and that made the whole thing look out of shape.

They were so misshapen that no two looked alike. They looked like a truck or tractor had run over them. In fact when the war ended, all that was produced in this giant factory complex was two small drill presses that were crated and ready to go.

I am convinced that the only place to put prisoners of war is on a farm, where they would probably work hard to produce their own food. Putting them in a factory similar to this is just inviting trouble.

There was one instance at the factory, where it appeared that a young Japanese group leader had developed an obvious friendship with one of the American prisoners whom he supervised. They were always talking and laughing and it was easy to see that the Japanese civilian was cultivating this friendly relationship. One day they were playing some sort of hand game and the American constantly won. As they played the smile on the Jap's face disappeared and eventually became very grim. Before long he could not stand losing any longer so without provocation or warning started slapping the American unmercifully. The American was utterly taken by surprise, but had to stand there and take the beating. You can be sure that this ended the friendship and in the future prisoners were leary of any Japanese that acted friendly. They could not be trusted.

Besides American POWs and Japanese workers there were many Chinese around as well. The Chinese were of the coolie class, and all of their work was on the outside. It appeared that their work was primarily hauling things in and out of the factory with most of the stuff coming in.

Hauling was done on a two-wheel cart, with a small flat bed pulled by a small Siberian pony. The two wheels had rubber tires and were undoubtedly the same as those found on automobiles.

The Chinese and the Americans got along very well. They called us big nose and we called them little nose, Da Beezer and Sho Beezer (big and little nose in Chinese). This spelling is probably wrong, but that is what it sounded like.

I thought that I had gone a long time without a bath, but it was nothing compared to the Chinese bath schedule. They took two baths in a lifetime, one when they were born and one when they died. They all looked dark skinned, but that was not their true color. You could see that they all needed a good scrubbing with soap and water, not only their clothes but their bodies as well.

One day at the factory some of the men grabbed a small Chinese boy and over his protests gave him a good face washing. It was surprising to see how fair skinned he was. The Chinese that I am referring to here were the so-called coolies. They were extremely poor and had problems just trying to survive. They do not have adequate facilities for washing clothes and bathing. To them in the bitter cold climate of Manchuria, it was better to stay dirty than freeze to death trying to stay clean.

Once contact was made with the Chinese and trust between us established, wheeling and dealing started. The Chinese would buy anything that you had stolen and now wanted to dispose of and had the money to pay cash for it.

They preferred things like tires, small electric motors, wire, tools anything that was not too bulky. Apparently they were masters at dealing in the black market and good at getting it out of the gate without being caught.

I was not involved in this activity, but some of the men made thousands of yen at it. With the money they turned around and bought medicine from the Chinese and such things as cigarettes and tobacco. Really there was not a lot to buy and having money did not help a person very much. With money came gambling and gambling brought problems. People without money gambled with food hoping to win money and then turn around and buy more food. There was only so much food to go around so if a person had more, because of his winnings it meant less for someone else. Some of the men were so far in debt that they had to declare bankruptcy. They had lost up to two or three months of their future rations and by then the winners wanted to collect.

That is when some of the officers stepped in and acted as trustees. The bankrupt person had to swear off gambling and promised to pay off his debt a little at a time. Perhaps at the rate of one or two bowls of soup a week or something similar.

Besides Americans in our camp, there were about 100 British, Australian and New Zealand troops with us. All of these men were captured at the fall of Singapore. They were in excellent shape because they were not subjected to the same kind of treatment that we were. When Singapore fell, and the Japanese moved in, they were confined to their barracks, but allowed to go out in small groups to buy things in the city. None of their personal items were taken, and they were left with their belongings intact. All they had to give up was their weapons. They had their uniforms, shoes, hats, coats and anything else that a British soldier would have. Apparently the Japanese did not hate the British as they hated the Americans. Because they were in better shape, none died.

I mentioned earlier about the lice problem and the difficulty of staying clean. To attempt to solve the problem most of the men kept their heads shaved, or I should say clipped, because that is what it was. There were a few who let their hair grow long. One guy in particular had long, curly red hair. Usually he stood out like a beacon among the baldies. This long hair came after we moved to our new location and keeping clean was much easier. When I had mine cut, I was always wondering, should I have it cut again now. What if the war should end suddenly and I had to go home bald? Embarrassing as it would be, it did not keep me from getting mine clipped time after time.

★ 13 ★

New Camp

I don't know how long we stayed at our first prison camp, but one day we were told that we would be moved to a new location. It was about a half mile from the factory and supposedly built by MKK.

When I first saw it, it reminded me of something like Alcatraz, a prison for criminals. The place was surrounded by a high brick wall with much higher guard towers at each corner. The wall was further heightened by many strands of barbed wire. Additionally, there were barbed-wire fences on the inside of the prison separated from each other by a distance of four to six feet. These fences were positioned about eight or ten feet from the brick wall. Guards constantly walked between the fences and the wall, twenty-four hours a day, and the high corner towers were also manned for the same length of time. There would be no escape from this place.

When we entered the gates of this prison, we were not allowed to go to our quarters immediately. We were stopped in an open area, where we were to be searched by eight or ten Japanese guards. This time they were not fooling around, and apparently felt that they were not going to let a single contraband item get into this camp.

I had never been seriously searched with the compass on me, since being searched on our march out of Bataan, but now things looked bad. Now I had no way of disposing of it, and I thought surely I would be caught. Some of the other men had musette bags similar to mine, and I could see that the guards were reaching way down into the small partition that held my compass. I decided my only possible way out of

135

this dilemma was to remove it from its hiding place and try hiding it elsewhere on me. I thought about putting it in my mouth, but it had about a 10 inch cord on it, and I was afraid the cord would show or I would be spotted stuffing the cord in my mouth.

We were being stripped naked and every item of clothes searched. When my time came in desperation I cupped it in my hand and with that hand started to unbutton my shirt. I removed the shirt and held it out to the guard to search, but still holding on to it with the compass hand. He went over it thoroughly and now wanted me to remove my pants.

As the guards searched items of clothes they threw them behind after being satisfied that nothing was there. So instead of letting the guard have my shirt, I threw it behind him myself and with the shirt went my compass. When I saw that the compass was not exposed and was covered by the shirt, I felt like a person reprieved from the gallows. I had lucked out and gotten away with it again.

I wasn't the only one that got contraband through. As I was picking up my clothes here comes more thrown next to mine and what do you know? Out pops an American flag. It had been tightly rolled and when it hit the ground it unrolled slightly. I was flabbergasted. Just as I picked up my compass and took off he did the same with his flag.

The inside of the prison was divided into two sections. One for the Japanese and one for the prisoners. A wall separated the two. The prison side contained several buildings, three of which were barracks. They were two-storied and constructed of brick. Each level had a hall running down the middle with compartments on both sides. The compartments had double decks and provided sleeping room for about forty or so people. The lower level was raised about six inches off the floor, which was typically Japanese.

I selected a lower level because I found what I thought was the perfect place for my compass. After the scare that I just went through, I did not want it to happen to me again. I discovered at the foot of my bunk there was a loose board.

It was one of the short boards that closed in the area between the floor and the lower bunks. I was able to remove this board and place it back in its proper position without difficulty, so I figured this was a good hiding place.

Again I removed the board and reached back as far as I could and placed the compass on one of the 2 x 6s that supported the floor. I closed the opening and now felt relieved. If the Japanese found it now, I could deny it was mine, wasn't I thoroughly searched when I entered? I could say maybe a Chinaman, who helped build this building put it there, hoping a prisoner would find it and use it in an escape. If it was found I would make up some kind of story.

To make sure that we did not bring lice into our new quarters, all of our clothes had to be boiled before entering. We now had a bath house in the place with two large tubs for boiling water. We had to dip our clothes in the hot water and then take them outside to dry.

It's a good thing this was the summer. A day or so later I took my first real bath since leaving Bataan and this was much better because the water was warm. It certainly beat the hosing down that we had at Taiwan.

The bathhouse had a concrete floor and in the center of the room stood the two large tubs. These tubs were not for entering, but only to provide hot water, which you poured over your head and body by means of fairly large wooden mugs. The only thing missing was towels for drying. I remember in the winter we had ice form on our bodies, when we ran from the bath house to the barracks. Most of our bathing now took place in the summer.

When I wrote earlier of the diseases that existed among the prisoners in the Philippines, I forgot to mention that we also had much scurvy and something else called Guam blisters. They were like a raw sore without a scab. They started as a small blister, which would not heal, but kept getting bigger and bigger. Since there was no medication to cure them, they would eat away the entire layer of skin leaving the flesh below exposed.

As the blister grew and devoured more skin, no scab formed, which made for an ugly looking sore. Where the good skin was being eaten away, there was always a small rim of pus. Some of these 'blisters' got as large as a silver dollar and some of the prisoners had several at one time.

I was lucky and did not have one, but did have a very large ringworm on my stomach. It was about as big as a saucer and getting larger by the day.

I am reminded about the Guam blisters, because I remembered seeing the terrible scars left by these sores now that the men were naked and washing off and the scars could be seen. They were fortunate now, however, because for some reason or other the blisters cured themselves in the cold weather.

We also left our old lice covered mattresses at our first camp and were given new ones here. We were given the mattress bag and had to fill it with hay or straw. I believe that it was rice straw and it came from a large pile that the Japanese brought in. From here on out the lice problem was essentially licked, but we were not pest free, because here came the fleas.

They only showed up in great numbers at night, but then it was by the hundreds. They were actually a lot more aggravating than lice. Their bite was also a lot more painful, and they made it almost impossible to sleep at night. It reached a point where our underwear looked like it was made from polka-dotted material, when in fact it was spotted with dry blood. Our mattress cover was also similarly soiled. Washing did not remove the spots only lightened them somewhat.

Even though we were in much better quarters our food had not improved, so we still had much sickness and some dying still. Tuberculosis now was killing people and beri beri was still prevalent. The beri beri was the dry type, and it was not killing any one, but it caused a great deal of pain and misery for some.

One poor person had it so bad that he would soak his feet for hours in a bucket of snow and ice. When it melted he would have someone go outside and refill his bucket. He even slept, or tried to sleep, with his feet hanging over the edge of his bunk in a bucket of ice. The feet of a person with beri beri felt like hot coals, and I imagine the heat generated was enough to keep them from freezing while being soaked.

In the summertime it was a different story. There was no snow or ice, so a person had to suffer. One of my friends had an especially bad case of beri beri; his suffering could be relieved by his being put to sleep. A stronger person would grab him around the chest and give a hard squeeze and out he would go. He could then sleep for hours.

Another person had dry beri beri so badly that he consented to be taken to a place in Mukden, where the nerves to his feet were severed. It apparently relieved his pain, but his feet now looked floppy to me like he did not have good control of them anymore.

By now my main problem was with my teeth. I had developed bad cavities in two back teeth, and they hurt constantly. When we fell out in the morning to be counted and sent off to the factory, those who felt sick could move out to a line in front, where the Jap officer of the day looked you over. If he felt that you were sufficiently sick he could let you stay in, and if he thought you were not that bad off, he would send you back to the group going to work.

I tried many, many times to stay in to have my teeth pulled, but I was always turned back. The Jap on duty would look in my mouth and say no!

I finally got them pulled much later, which still makes me cringe when I think about it. Once in a blue moon we would get a day off because it was a Japanese holiday. So when the next holiday arrived, I decided to have it done. We had a small dispensary in one of the buildings, and that is where I headed.

I found another person there waiting for the same thing. Pretty soon two Japanese came in and wanted to know what was wrong with us, so we opened our mouths and showed them what our problem was. There was no such thing as filling teeth, just pulling them.

Since the person with me was there before me, I let him go first. They sat him down on a chair and started working on him.

I could hear him groan from time to time and wondered why it was taking so long.

Soon I saw one Jap pulling and the other holding on to a head with the head now really groaning as if in horrible pain. The Japs pulled and pulled, but never did get the tooth out. They finally let him up and then turned to me.

By now I was wondering if my teeth really hurt as much as I thought they did. Well, I had reached a point where I could not retreat so I sat down in the chair. One of the Japanese reached for an instrument, and I instinctively opened my mouth. He reached in and I immediately felt this horrible pain. I thought good it is finally out. In another second or two more pain just like the first, and more, and more.

What was happening was that the Japanese was not pulling yet, he was just cutting the gum away from the tooth so that he could reach way down on it to get a good grip for pulling.

Having teeth pulled at new prison camp in Mukden

They did this, I found out later, to prevent the tooth from breaking into several parts when being extracted. This had happened to several prisoners and they were left with parts of roots deeply imbedded in their jaw bone. They were now worse off than before.

To get back to my tooth, luckily it finally came out without any problem. The pulling was less painful than the cutting. I forgot to mention that there was no novocaine or other pain killer provided when teeth were pulled.

Later on I had the second one extracted by the same process, but it was less painful, because I was pretty well tipsy from drinking alcohol when I went to have it done. I was afraid that the Japanese would smell the whiskey on my breath, but they did not. The dispensary was permeated with the smell of alcohol to begin with so this helped to conceal the odor in my mouth.

Although the new barracks that we were now in were a big improvement over the old that we came from in some aspects, in others they were not.

To look at the heating system in the new buildings you would have to say it looked great. Big Russian-type stoves called Pitchkas on each floor and their size implied that one alone could heat the entire building without any problem. That was not the case, however. The big round stove was mostly solid brick with a very small fire box. The object was to burn a small fire for several days, which eventually warmed the mass of bricks, which in turned warmed the room.

This sounds great, but since we were only allowed one scuttle of coal per day, it was not enough to begin to warm the huge stoves. Also the so-called coal was mostly slate, and very difficult to light. About one half would burn and the other half not. We soon gave up even trying to light the stoves so the barracks stayed cold in the winter. By cold I mean very cold. In fact the inside of the barrack's walls looked like a freezer that needed defrosting. There was a good inch or more of frost on the walls that lasted throughout the very long winters.

I mentioned earlier that I worked inside of the factory at MKK, but sometime later I got an outside job. I liked it better, because we were not as closely supervised. Our job was to straighten out a large pile of used lumber by pulling nails and separating it into its various kinds and sizes. After it was free of nails it was then stacked in neat piles. The Chinese would come with their carts from time to time. On occasions it was to dump more lumber on the pile and at other times take stacked wood and carry it off. We didn't know where it came from or where it was going. That was not our business.

Remember, we are still hungry and are always looking for extra food. The first thing that we got from the Chinese coming in our lumber yard was fried grasshopper. It was fried crisp and very tasty. With it was some fried bell pepper which gave it flavor.

We soon learned that the Chinese could get for us such things as Irish potatoes, squash, carrots, turnips, etc. What we needed was a place to store it to keep it out of sight of the Japanese.

We looked around our area and found nearby several large round cement culverts that had been stored in a group. Each culvert was three feet across and four feet long and was exactly what we were looking for. We would bury it in our lumberyard and cover the top with boards in the summer time and boards and snow in the winter.

It did not take us long to dig a hole, steal a culvert without being seen, and bury it. We were now ready to seriously deal with the Chinese. Before long we had a few Irish potatoes, a small pumpkin or squash and some carrots. Unfortunately, we never did get to eat any of the stuff, because we were waiting for winter to come so that we could cook it.

I should mention that where we were in Manchuria all water had to be boiled before drinking and all vegetables had to be cooked on account of disease. All gardens were fertilized with human waste, which meant all produce was contaminated, which is why nothing could be eaten raw.

With winter coming on we knew that we would be allowed to light a fire in the small stove that we had in our shack. With a fire we could then cook our food, if we were not caught that is.

Our shack was a small building where we could hang up our coats in the summer and spend some time warming up in the winter. The winters were so cold that a person could not be made to stay out all day without the person freezing to death, especially with the shoes and clothes that we had. I forgot to mention that there were eight of us that worked in the lumberyard.

As a kid in school I remember the teachers used to tell us how in China, if a baby girl was born she was abandoned and left to die. I never really believed it and felt they were only trying to raise money for the missionaries by making us feel sorry for the babies. In Manchuria, however, we found it to be true. Dead babies were found on several occasions in the factory trash pile, and we assumed they were Chinese.

For a very long time now we had had no news about the progress of the war. The Japanese kept telling us that before long they would be sitting in the White House in Washington. None of us believed this propaganda, but why was it taking the U.S. so long to beat the Japanese? We did not, or at least I did not, know about Pearl Harbor, and maybe it was a good thing not knowing. Had we known I know that our morale would have sunk to the bottom of our toes.

Eventually we began to learn what was going on far away in the South Pacific in a roundabout way. One of the men was assigned to work in the administration office of the factory, where the Japanese company executives also worked.

I don't know what our man did for the Japanese, but he certainly did a lot for the prisoners. The Japanese in the office got an occasional newspaper, which they trashed after it was read. Our man was able to retrieve one once in a while and smuggle it into camp.

He had a unique way of doing it, and it was never discovered. Somehow he had hollowed out the heel of his shoe and it had sufficient room to jam in parts of the newspaper. The paper was not like the kind that we have in the U.S., but was much smaller in size and printed on much thinner paper.

The newspapers were in Japanese, but that did not matter because we had a British or Australian officer in camp that could read it very well. When a paper came in, it was taken to him to read and digest, and a short while later we had a news report.

We would gather to hear it in one barracks and had American guards posted at each entrance to make sure the Japanese did not discover what was going on. In their paper, the Japanese never admitted losing a battle or abandoning a base or position. They always won, but a person with a little common sense could see from following the news that something was not right. One day they were pounding the American troops from bases on such and such an island, but a few weeks later they were either bombing enemy troops on that same island or being attacked by planes from it. They were being pushed back, but would not admit it to their people.

So far I have not mentioned anything, or very little, about our thoughts of home and family. It was a personal thing with everyone and was little, if ever, discussed, but you can be sure that it was on everyone's mind.

If others were like me, and I am sure most were, you thought about your poor parents back home almost every night, and knew how they were suffering, not knowing where you were or how you were, or even not sure if you were alive or dead. This must have been agony to them. The same could be said of brothers and sisters and wives and children.

I always felt that the prisoners who suffered the most mentally were the ones with wives and children back home. I know it was extra hard on them, but they were few in number. Most of the men were young and not yet married.

What would bring on memories of home and freedom at

night was the sound of train whistles far off in the distance. It made me think of the lovely train trip through the Feather River Valley, when we were on our way to San Francisco. It made you realize how precious freedom was and also made you wonder if you would ever know it again.

I know every one enjoyed going to sleep at night, and if you dreamed it was usually always the same, but it left you extremely depressed the next day. In most dreams you were at last freed from prison camp and back in the States and feeling euphoric.

Free, free, free again-how wonderful, but the shock of awakening was so heartbreaking when you found out you were still in prison. I believe these dreams actually did more harm than good. Even so, they came back time and time again. There was no getting away from them. No, the people back home were not forgotten, and we knew they had not forgotten us.

Our treatment now was not bad, and I think the reason for it was now we were guarded entirely by Manchurian guards. With the exception of camp officers, most lower-rank Japanese soldiers were gone and presumably sent south to help in the fighting.

When we were punished now it was primarily because of something we did, that we knew was wrong, so there was some justification for it. The only bad thing, however, was when some one messed up, the entire camp suffered the consequences.

Our biggest troublemaker was probably alcohol. No, we were not issued alcohol, but all of the Japanese workers at the factory were from time to time. It was issued to them at their lunch break so they had to take it back to their work station for storage until leaving for home at night. Between lunch break and quitting is when the stuff disappeared. When the Japanese went for their whiskey most of it was gone. You can imagine the commotion. Losing it once seemed bad enough, but it happened time after time. Of course each time we were punished, primarily by being made to stand at attention for long periods of time. This was no big deal in the summer time, but in the winter it could be brutal, since it was always done at night. No coats allowed, of course.

Another time the Japanese discovered an American flag that had been smuggled in. We always had prisoners guarding at each door, when the flag was displayed, but one time a guard left his post and the Japs walked in on us. Needless to say, that did not go over too well.

Before I get too far ahead of the whiskey episodes, I must explain what actually happened to it, the whiskey that is. It could not be consumed at the factory so a method had to found to get it into camp.

The method wasn't long in coming, and it was ingenious. During their lunch break, the Japanese girls that worked in the front office went outside for exercise, which for the most part was playing volleyball.

Somehow some of the men got hold of some of these balls and pulled out their bladders. These bladders were excellent containers for liquids, such as whiskey and were also ideal for smuggling it into camp. Volleyball bladders are flat, and when partially filled and placed in the pit of your stomach, are virtually impossible to detect under clothing when being searched. If touched they felt soft and giving just like a stomach.

Not every effort succeeded in getting whiskey into the camp, however. Some days we were completely stripped when searched which meant little or nothing got through. As I described before, the search was done by six or eight guards and could go very slowly, if they were being very thorough.

Men carrying in alcohol would stand in the back of the line to see what kind of searching was taking place. If it was haphazard, as it could be at times, just a quick going over by hand, then they gambled and went on through. However, if the search appeared too thorough then they got rid of their loot. It was easy to dispose of because it was almost dark when we arrived back in camp, and another thing, we were right against an outside wall, which came in handy. Under near dark conditions it was easy to sail the bladder of whiskey over the wall without being seen. Once over the wall it landed in an open area very close to the road that we used daily to go to and from work. We could see the bladders lying there, but no longer could get to them. The Japanese never did discover how the liquor got into our camp.

Not everyone that stole whiskey at the factory was brave enough to bring it in, or maybe did not have access to bladders, so they hired someone else to do the job for them. For a price someone would do it. Toward the end of the war most of the Manchurian guards were bought off. If you had a small item, such as a pack of cigarettes, you could give it to a guard at the factory in the morning, tell him where your bunk was, and that night find it under your mattress. By this time I think they realized that the Japanese were losing the war, and they wanted to be looked on with favor when the end came. That was not it entirely though, because we did have to pay them for their help.

Besides stealing and scrounging some of the men had other useful talents. What I thought was the most impressive of all was a jacket made by one of the men. It was made from a British blanket and looked tailor made. Some beautiful smoking pipes were also made. Some were even crooked stemmed with the pipe bowl made from a wood knot to make it resemble real briar. The pipe stems were made from a hard rubber that was picked up (stolen) somewhere in the factory. The one bad thing about having a pipe was that there was no good pipe tobacco around.

The Chinese all smoked a pipe, but instead of the bowl being wood it was made out of metal. The stem was made from a piece of bamboo. Their pipes were not at all like ours, especially in size. Their metal bowl was about as large as the end of your little finger and held a very small quantity of tobacco. Their tobacco was also different in that it was as fine as dust. We surmised that these were opium pipes with the opium being in the tobacco dust. Although the Chinese apparently used drugs freely, none to my knowledge, were ever used by the prisoners.

Earlier I talked about having a large ringworm on my stomach. Well, I finally got rid of it. A friend of mine had a pipe and a bit of tobacco to go with it. When a pipe is smoked, there is always a concentration of nicotine that develops in the stem around the pipe filter if it has one. This nicotine is like a dark, thick gum.

Thinking it might work on curing my ring worm, I decided to give it a try. I asked my friend to save his pipe cleanings for me, which he did, and I started applying it to my stomach. I am happy to say it worked and in four or five weeks the ring worm was cured.

Besides clothes and pipes, which most of us could not make, there were some things that most of us could make. A lot of us made our own needles for darning our clothes and most made extra shoes to wear in the summer time. Instead of being real shoes, they were more like sandals or so-called clogs. They were wooden soles with a strap across the toe area to hold them on.

It took some getting used to, but once learned they were very practical. Most were made from a plain, flat piece of wood and were as simple as could be, but others were more fancy. The fancy ones were cut out to resemble a foot print with a heel and carved arch support added for looks and possibly comfort. Mine were as plain as you can make them. The hard part was finding a suitable toe strap.

I forgot to mention that when talking about bringing in contraband to the camp, that a signal had been worked out between the camp and factory to let us know what Japanese officer of the day was on duty. When the one that we called the Bull was on, no one tried smuggling anything in, because he was terrible and would beat you severely if you were caught. When he was on, we could be sure that we would be completely stripped when searched.

On the other hand we had some that were very lenient, so

it was important to know who was on duty. If the Bull was on, the signal was something visible from the factory hanging out of one of the barracks. There was always someone in camp who took on this responsibility, and this is another activity that the Japanese never discovered.

I should point out that all of the prisoners did not work at MKK factory. A large number were moved out to work in a factory somewhere else, still in Manchuria, but I am not sure where. It was probably somewhere in the vicinity of Mukden, because when the war ended they were returned to our camp for evacuation. We also had people that stayed in our camp, but worked in another factory nearby. One of the places was a leather-tanning factory and I don't recall what the other was.

For the most part the prisoners got along very well with each other, but there were instances when conflicts arose and fights broke out between individuals. One was between a Limey and an American. We were talking about drinking beer and the American said, "Gee, but I would like a bottle of ice cold beer right now."

The British guy said, "No, a cool beer would be much tastier." The American said, "You don't know what you are talking about. The colder the better."

The Limey said, "Below a certain degree of coldness you can't taste the beer."

The American said, "Warm beer tastes like piss." The Limey replied, "Bull —," and that's when it started. By now they were so mad at each other that they started a fist fight. We let them go at it for a while, and then broke it up. They later realized how foolish they were.

There was another good fight in the barracks one night over a bun. This was between two Americans. One guy said that the other owed him a bun and would not pay up.

Several months before the war ended the Japanese put every one to digging foxholes. They were not for us but for the Japanese. Some were at the factory and some on the Japanese side of the camp. None were on our side.

When this work started, we knew that the Japanese were now expecting possible air raids, and we were excited because the war was getting closer. It wasn't too much longer after we finished digging all of the foxholes that we were required to cover them over. They were covered with heavy timbers and then further covered with a large mound of dirt. This told us that the Japanese were taking a pounding somewhere, which in our minds was great.

At about this same time the Japanese were becoming rather aggressive, and there was a definite change in their attitude and treatment of us. We now had to really watch what we were doing, and if we did anything illegal, make sure we were not caught. Some of the men were caught, however, and suffered the consequences.

I recall once it involved alcohol and an innocent person was put in the guardhouse for someone else's doings. Liquor was found in his bunk, but it was not his. The real owner would not step forward and claim it, which was to be expected, otherwise he would have hidden it in his own possessions. Except for minor incidents, things had run smoothly up to this point, but things were changing.

Before this we did have it relatively good for a while, especially when the Japanese said that they were going to pay those of us that worked. We were going to get a small amount of pay each day, which we would then be able to spend at a commissary that they were going to open in camp.

They finally did open the store, but the merchandise was very meager. As I remember, there was soap, toothbrushes, combs and things of that nature, and that was it. The soap and toothbrushes were great, but who needed a comb? not me, for one, with my bald head.

I don't recall receiving money, but supposedly they had your earnings in a ledger and would subtract your purchase from that amount. We soon found out why they did this for a while.

Apparently they had consented to let Red Cross representatives in for a visit, and they wanted things to look good.

The day they arrived we were at work, and the few people that remained in camp did not get to see or speak to them. We never did know what their nationality was, but I am sure they went back home greatly impressed.

The prisoners were being paid, lived in new quarters, fed three times a day and even had a store in which to spend their earnings. They should have come back in a few weeks, however, because that is about how long the store lasted. No one really cared because it meant nothing to us anyway. We much preferred doing business in the black market.

★ 14 ★

Air Raids

One morning, shortly after we had gone to work, air-raid sirens started going off all over the city, and everyone became very excited, especially the Japanese.

We were quickly rounded up and made to double time back to camp. This time we were not searched, but sent immediately to our barracks and told to stay inside.

We could still hear sirens going off in all directions. We had not been in our barracks very long when the Japanese came back and said everyone outside and in the yard.

Our yard was probably about 150 to 200 feet long and perhaps 100 wide, more or less. When everyone was out the Japanese made us lie down and then took off probably for their foxholes.

It wasn't long before we could see a large formation of heavy bombers headed our way. They were very high up and each left a streak in the sky that extended for many miles behind it. It was a beautiful sight and we felt proud and excited. It had to be American planes and the war reached Manchuria.

We watched them slowly come our way, but the Japanese also saw them coming and sent up fighter planes to intercept them, which was a mistake. From the ground it looked like a swarm of mosquitoes going after a flock of geese and the comparison is good, because that is about how effective the Jap fighters were.

From the ground we could see flashes of fire coming from the bombers and see Japanese planes go plunging down in smoke. Just about then you could hear the roar of the guns

152

from the bombers as the sound reached the ground. Time after time the Japs moved in, but the results were the same. Japs going down in flame and no apparent damage to the bombers. What a fight!

We had seen dog fights on Bataan, but nothing as exciting as this, especially since we were now winning for a change. The Japanese soon broke off their attack, and that is when their anti-aircraft guns opened up. Puffs of smoke from exploding shells now filled the air, but the bombers kept coming.

I would like to interrupt the writing about this attack at this point and mention that our prison camp was in the middle of a heavily industrialized area, which was against international rules of war. We should not have been imprisoned where we were.

Right next to us was an ammunition factory and a short distance behind us was a tank factory. We were also very close to an airplane factory and a major rail yard. There were numerous military targets for the Americans to bomb, and, unfortunately, we were right in the middle of them.

Still lying on my back, I kept my eyes on the bombers and was impressed by the large number in the formation, about eighteen or twenty as I recall. Pretty soon I could see the silver flashes of released bombs and in another few seconds saw the sky filled with hundreds of bombs hurtling down on us and all making their typical loud swishing sound. I knew they could not miss and they did not.

Three of the bombs from the plane on the outside of the formation hit our camp, and the destruction was horrible. One of the bombs landed near the high brick wall that surrounded our compound and knocked a big chunk out of its top. The next bomb fell right in the yard where we were lying and instantly killed nineteen of us and severely wounded many more. The third bomb was incendiary and fell on one of our barracks and set it on fire. It was a tragedy. Here we were, after so very long a time, excited beyond belief at watching our side win for a change and look what

New camp bombed by American B-29 planes

happened! We could hardly believe it, but we were now being killed by our own bombs.

Even though I was within twenty or so feet from the bomb, I was not hurt. As I looked up I saw men blackened from the blast, try to rise but fall back terribly wounded or dead. I was only a few feet from the ring of death that surrounded the bomb crater, but luckily it was just far enough.

By now prisoners that were not hurt were rushing to assist those that were. The Japanese came into the yard, but they were told to leave which they did. The wounded were taken to our dispensary and treated, as well as they could be with the medicine that was on hand, which was very little. The dead were removed, and I am not sure what happened to their bodies. I suspect that they were also buried in the graveyard on the hill with the others, but I am not certain.

After it was all over, I could recall in my mind exactly what happened. I remember seeing the left wing of the end bomber tip up very slightly as it released its bombs. When this happened it threw its bombs slightly to the left of its target and right on top of us. The unsteadiness of the plane was probably caused by an erratic air current or from the concussion of bursting antiaircraft shells near it.

The American bombers may have inadvertently killed some of their own men on the ground, but they definitely also brought death and destruction upon the enemy. Their target was the ammunition factory just off to one side of our compound, and it. went up with a tremendous roar. As far as I know it was completely destroyed. I recall seeing an antiaircraft gun positioned on top of one of the buildings, and I thought, What a stupid place to have it, and it was. They were blown sky high with everything else.

I still can't get over how the bomb that fell in the middle of us did its killing. Of course, where the bomb hit many were killed outright, but there was a ring of prisoners that survived inside an outer ring of dead and wounded. Luckily, I was a little beyond this last ring. If the Japanese had let us dig foxholes for ourselves, as well as for them, then our casualties would have been greatly reduced. Even now they would not let us have them.

No more bombers appeared for about a week, but one day the sirens starting screaming again, and it was as before, double time back to camp.

Again, we were not allowed inside but made to lie outside on the ground, where the bombs had killed before. Pretty soon, coming from the same direction as the first attack, was another very large group of American planes high in the sky. With their streaming con-trails they could be seen for miles.

I have to be honest and say this time we were not as happy to see them as we were before. They kept coming, and it soon became obvious that they were heading directly for us, as opposed to the first flight, which looked like it was slightly off to one side.

This group was about as large as the first: eighteen to twenty planes. As before, when they got near the city, the Japanese sent up fighter planes again, but this time it was twin-engine attack planes with just a few fighters.

When the fighting in the air started, it was just like before, a flash of fire from the heavy bombers, Japanese planes going down in flames or smoking, then the sound of gunfire reaching us below. The attack planes of the Japanese did no better than the fighters and they eventually pulled away.

That is when the antiaircraft opened up but appeared ineffective. The mass of American planes kept coming, and now there was no doubt that they would pass directly over us. As always, I was on my back looking up to see if or when bombs would be released, and sure enough this time there was no if about it.

I could see the hundreds of silvery flashes appear just as the bombs were released and the precise time of their release, a little before they were overhead meant that we were facing grave danger again.

Still on my back, I kept looking and what I saw still sends shivers up my spine. Literally hundreds of bombs were bearing down on us with their deadly sound, and I figured, this is it. There was no way that so many bombs could miss us. Before I had time to flip over on my stomach, they were exploding, shaking the ground like an earthquake, but were not exploding on us. They had skimmed just over our camp and hit a factory that was just behind us. What a scare!

When the Japanese bombed us with heavy bombers in the Philippines, it was usually with eight or ten planes and they dropped thirty or forty bombs total at one time. Not so with the Americans. They dropped bombs by the hundreds.

All the Japanese in the factory could talk about now was the American, nee, jew, coos, that's Japanese for B-29's.

They were deadly afraid of them, and they had good reason to be. Raids over Mukden continued for quite a while, but none gave us the scare that the first two did. Of course, these raids played havoc with our work. Every time American planes appeared, it was back to camp we went. After the raid, back to the factory. These were exciting times.

One day the sirens went off again, and it was back to camp we go. We were in our usual position in camp, lying down on the ground. We kept watching the sky and waiting to see planes when all of a sudden a huge formation went scream-ing over our heads no more than eight or 10,000 feet high, if that high. I don't know why they came in so low this time, but it turned out to be a mistake.

One of the planes took a direct hit from antiaircraft fire and exploded in midair. After the explosion, the biggest pieces of the plane seen falling to the ground were its engines. The rest was fragments. We heard from the Chinese at the factory that this raid destroyed the railway yard.

A few days after this last raid the Japanese started taking soup from our kitchen and walking out of the camp with it. We became suspicious because we knew that the Japanese would not be eating the stuff themselves, but were probably feeding it to other prisoners. That's when it dawned on us that there must have been survivors on the one plane that was shot down.

I had nothing to do with the next part of this story but wished I had, it was so ingenious and clever. After sending out soup daily for several weeks the men in our galley decided to see if they could somehow make contact with whomever was eating it. They came up with a brilliant scheme, and it worked.

I think I mentioned before that our soup was distributed in wooden buckets (resembled ice cream buckets), and the buckets had a wooden lid to keep the stuff from splashing out or getting cold. The lid had a good sturdy wooden han-dle, which probably added weight to the lid as well as allow for easy removal.

The sturdy wooden handle turned out to be what the men

were looking for. Somehow they hollowed it out and fixed it so that it could be slipped on and off. Now they began sending messages. I am not sure how long this took but eventually someone found the messages because they were now being removed.

The big question was: Is it the Japanese or is it possibly other prisoners? To try to determine which it was, a series of questions was asked and return answers were requested. Questions went out, and answers came back and finally men in our camp decided that the Japanese could not possibly answer some of the questions asked so they assumed, and rightly so, that we were feeding and communicating with fellow Americans.

Now messages did not have to be as cautiously worded as before, and we soon found out that we were right in our original assumption.

These were men (fourteen, as I remember) who had survived the blowing up of their B-29 bomber and were now being held captive in a house within sight of our camp.

They said that they did not know of our prison camp and in actuality it was marked on their maps as a 'must get' target. This wasn't terribly reassuring, but they did pass on more cheering information than that. They said that Japan was being defeated all over the Pacific, and it appeared that the war should not last too very much longer. By the action in the sky we had already come to assume that. They also told us that they were flying out from the island of Guam.

Writing about passing notes reminds me that we once had an occasion to pen a few words that hopefully would eventually reach our family. These notes, I believe, were given to the Red Cross people that came into camp that one time.

Instead of delivering the written notes, I believe some of these were aired over the radio somewhere and whoever picked up the messages could try to get them to the appropriate families.

I don't believe that my message got home, but a friend's message did. He mentioned something about his friend from Eunice was with him and was fine. Whoever picked up the message had my last name misspelled, but I believe this information did reach my family. In this same message he passed on a coded part, which said that another person from his hometown had died. The code was in the form of a little jingle that was not censored.

There was always the possibility, we felt, that when the war was over, or about over and the Japanese realized that they had lost, they may decide to execute all of us instead of letting us go free. I personally thought about it and even had a plan in mind if and when such an event would take place.

My plan was this: The area back of the barracks was not accessible to us because it was very close to the wire fences and brick wall that enclosed our prison camp. From the inside back wall of our barracks, to a position beyond and outside of the brick wall was a distance of only about forty feet or so.

I felt it could be quickly and easily tunneled if need be. The ground that we were on was 100 percent sand, which meant easy digging, but the problem that it presented was keeping the tunnel from caving in. I felt that we could rip up a few boards under our mattresses and use them as supports. I don't know if my plan would have ever gotten off the ground, but luckily we never had to try it. When generals and admirals and other high-ranking personnel were brought into camp, I felt that we were much less likely to be killed.

When the Philippine Islands were finally invaded by the Americans, and the Japanese started pulling out, they loaded all of their American prisoners on ships with the intention of taking them out as well.

I could never understand why this was done, because surely it had no strategic significance. It was terribly destructive to our prisoners, however, because these fleeing ships were prime targets for our fighters and dive bombers.

Many were sunk and with them went a very large number of our men. The prisoners that survived and made it to shore were recaptured and put back on ships going out. Many were sunk again and more men died. Some had as many as three ships sunk under them before they were safely out of danger. I mention this incident because a lot of these survivors were sent to our camp in Manchuria.

After numerous raids on Mukden by American planes, their attacks ceased. I assume that their mission had been accomplished, and they had destroyed enough to severely hurt the Japanese war effort. Apparently a lot of Japanese industry that was war related was moved up into Manchuria, the Japs thinking that it would be safe from attack by the Americans, but it was not.

After three or four air raids by the Americans, the Japanese realized that their fighter planes were not effective against the fire power of B-29s so they tried a new tactic to protect their factories from being destroyed.

Since they could not stop the bombers in the air, they decided they could confuse them by hiding their targets on the ground. Now when air-raid sirens went off, instead of sending fighter and attack planes up to intercept the Americans, they lit smoke fires all over the city, which blackened the sky before the bombers arrived. I don't know if this was a big help to the Japanese or not. It may have saved some of their planes, however, because now they flew close to the ground, hidden from above by the thick layer of black smoke.

It was about then, our third year of imprisonment, that the Japanese started bringing in a whole lot of new people. We now had generals by the dozens, who were American, English, Australian and Dutch, as well as dozens and dozens of colonels from these various countries, plus an untold number of lesser officers. I could not believe the number of high ranking officers that were captured by the Japanese. I heard that the Japs got thirteen of our generals when the Philippines fell.

After the officers, came the survivors of the ships that had been sunk by American planes. This is when we heard their horrible story. A few of these men were from my outfit, and I was so glad to see them. They seemed happy to see us as well. The high-ranking crowd did not come from prison camps in the Philippines, but from a camp near Harbin, Manchuria.

At our camp the officers probably had it worse than the enlisted men because they had no outside contacts where they could get cigarettes and extra food.

I remember one quartermaster general in particular who used to come around and bum smokes. He didn't really beg for them, but you could not finish a smoke without feeling sorry for him so we gave him a short butt on occasion.

I remember asking the general questions about the war, but he said we knew more about what was going on than he did because we were there doing the fighting and he wasn't. At least he was honest. As far as I could tell from what he told me, his big accomplishment was in peace time, when he convinced the army to go to long pants for its soldiers, instead of the breeches and leggings that it was issuing.

I found out much later from a camp roster I acquired, that besides the high-ranking military personnel now in our camp, we had some prominent civilian people as well. We had a British governor and chief justice from Singapore, I presume, and two governors from Dutch colonies. I might mention that we also had the generals that surrendered Bataan and Singapore. The only person missing was General Wainright. He had been with these people, but was now held alone somewhere in Manchuria.

★ 15 ★

Guardhouse

One morning when we arrived at the factory and headed for our work in the lumber yard, we noticed Japanese soldiers all over the place. They were running and crawling and obviously playing war. They were lying on the ground, hiding behind piles of lumber and some even on top of our neatly stacked piles. Not too far from them was an opposing force doing about the same thing.

We just ignored what was going on and walked right through them to get to our shack. We were in the process of hanging up our coats, when a Japanese officer burst in on us and he was Mad, Mad, Mad.

We didn't know what he was saying, but it undoubtedly had something to do with our ignoring his serious maneuvers. He chewed us out for awhile and finally left. We closed the door behind him and one of our group let out a loud laugh, after we thought that he was gone, but he wasn't. Apparently he was just outside our door waiting for such a response and back in he comes.

This time you could say he was foaming at the mouth because his raging voice was sending out as much saliva as sound. He had his saber out and was really furious this time. He lined us all up in our little shack and with his saber in his left hand, he started giving each one of us a hard punch in the mouth with his right. I was near the door on the end of the line and when I saw what was happening, I thought to myself, I am not going to let that bastard punch me in the mouth, so I slipped out. I knew if I got caught I would really get a beating, but I left anyway. Luckily I got away with it and

162

escaped this beating, but I had one coming when we arrived back in camp that night.

As I recall we had eight people who worked in the lumber yard and before the Jap officer left, he had our leader (a British sergeant) write down all our numbers, which he took with him.

During this encounter, we had a British prisoner with us, who should not have been there. He actually worked in the factory, but was goofing off in our shack. He got a smack in the mouth, but that was as far as it went because his number was not turned in, but mine was. He really would have been in big trouble had it been, so I imagine it was best that it was not.

As expected, when we arrived in camp that night, our numbers were called out, and we were made to stand aside as the rest of the men were searched and released to the barracks. Finally the Japanese officer of the day and his interpreter got back to us. He would question one of us for a while out of each others' hearing, and turn him over to a guard who would march him off to the guardhouse.

The guardhouse, or jail within a prison, was located just on the inside of the main gate. It could truly be called a guardhouse because it is where the Japanese guarding the prison entrance stayed and the place where punished prisoners were confined. Everyone knew where it was and did not want to be put in it, especially after hearing what it was like on the inside from some of those who had been there.

Finally it was my turn to be questioned. Through his interpreter, the Japanese officer asked me where I worked, and I told him. He wanted to know if I worked with the other men being questioned, and I said yes.

He then asked me what my number was, and I said, "Itchy, yon, son, coo."

Then he asked me if I thought that the Japanese officer at the factory had a right to hit us the way he did. I hesitated for a second, like I was pondering the question, then answered, "Well, I am not sure."

Just as soon as these words came out of my mouth, I knew

that I had answered wrong. But nothing happened, and I was questioned a bit further until the same question came up again.

"Did I think that the Japanese officer at the factory had the right to hit us the way he did?" For a second I was in a quandary. Should I just say, "Yes, sir" or should I repeat my first answer.

I decided maybe being consistent was the way to go, so I repeated my original answer, and that was a mistake. Almost instantly I was hit on the right side of my jaw with a closed fist, not by the officer, but by the interpreter.

From that point on he decided to slap me in the face as hard as he could. I think he really hurt his fist when he first hit me and that is why he slapped.

All the while you were being beaten, you were made to stand at attention. With this kind of beating, you don't give them the satisfaction of knowing you are hurt. You just don't let yourself fall down and moan. All I could think about was, you little S.O.B. if I could just get you alone under different circumstances, I would tear you apart.

After the beating stopped, I was thrown in the guard-house with the rest of the guys. The inside of my mouth was

Serving time in guardhouse

badly cut, and I swallowed blood for several days. My face was swollen, and I am sure that I had black eyes.

We had three different Japanese interpreters in our camp. The first was a graduate of some California university and could speak English a lot better than me. He really hated Americans, and possibly could have been one. He said Americans all thought that they were superior to the Japanese. He said we laughed and made fun of their clothes, shoes, customs, etc. but now we were going to pay for it.

His name was Noda, and he told us that he would be back in the States long before we would, when the war was over and I don't doubt that he was.

Another one of the interpreters, who came after Noda, was very good to us. He was from Hawaii, and unlike Noda, who was always looking for an excuse to punish us, he on many occasions overlooked actions that would have otherwise resulted in punishment.

The third interpreter, and the one that beat me, was a young Jap who came a few months before the war ended. I think he was a Kiss Ass, who was trying to impress the higher ups. When the war ended, I should have searched out this punk and done to him what he did to me, but our senior officers would not allow it.

I stayed in the guardhouse for about three weeks and was not let out until a week or two before the war ended. We were all released at the same time, I believe the reason for this was that the Japanese knew that the war was about over. Normally, there was a trial and a sentence for anyone that was sent to the guardhouse, but we had neither, unless the questioning and beating was my trial and the three weeks of confinement my sentence.

Many, many years later the person that did the laughing in our shack at the lumber yard came to one of the 27th Bomb Group conventions just to look me up and apologize for the misery that he caused us way back when. He was not from my outfit.

Conditions in the guardhouse were unbelievably cruel

and I hope I can explain exactly what it was like. It was built similar to our barracks except it had cells instead of separate sleeping quarters. There was a central hall with cells on either side. Each cell was about eight-feet wide and probably twelve-feet long with a very narrow slit trench for a latrine in a back corner. The floor was concrete and that was it, no bed, blanket, chair, or anything else.

There was a small opening on the back wall that could be called a window, but it was high up and tightly sealed with heavy boards. The bars that faced the central hall were made out of 4 x 4-inch pieces of lumber with about a three-inch spacing between them.

The cells were staggered so that you would not see anyone directly across from you when each of you stood in the center of your cell. You could, however, just barely see someone across from you if he got very close to the cell bars nearest you and you in turn got close to the cell bars nearest to him.

We were fed bread and water for three days and then soup the next with the soup coming twice a day instead of three times.

There was no heat in the cells; the one thing that I was thankful for was that it was not winter.

We were awakened at 5 o'clock in the morning and not let to lie down and rest or sleep until 11 o'clock at night.

While we were awake we had to stand at attention and a guard constantly walked the hallway to make sure that we did.

He walked slowly from one end to the other, but he was a fool if he thought that we really stayed at attention like we were supposed to.

Once he got a little past my cell, I relaxed until I heard him coming back. The partition between cells was solid so the guard could not see you until he was almost in front of you. There was no danger of him sneaking up on you either, because the heavy nails on the soles and heels of his shoes on the cement floor made a sound that could be heard a country mile away. I might add that the guard carried a rifle with a fixed bayonet, which was a standard practice for them, both in the guardhouse or outside.

The guardhouse was solitary confinement at its worst. I found the hardest thing to take was the boredom. You've heard the song "Time Goes by so Slowly"? Well, it certainly applied then.

Standing in one place, even if not at attention, can be a killer. I used to watch a spot of light that came in through a crack in the boarded window, and it almost drove me mad. I tried to ignore it but couldn't.

I would be made to get up in the morning at 5 o'clock, and several hours later, when there was sufficient light, the spot would appear. It first showed up on one side of my cell wall and then moved so terribly slowly across the other side until it finally disappeared. After it was gone, I knew I still had several more hours to go before I would get to rest. It was agony to watch and it was the same thing day after day after day. These were eighteen-hour days, and now I know why the one poor soul, who was held so long came out the way he did.

Although we were in different cells, and impossible as it may seem, we were able to communicate with each other. About a month or so before this incident that put us in the guardhouse took place, all of us learned the hand alphabet. One of the men knew it, and he was our teacher.

We practiced in the lumber yard and all became very good in very short order. We did not realize at the time that we would get to use it before too very long.

I mentioned earlier that our prison cells were staggered across the hall so that we could not see each other when standing at attention in the center of the cell.

The corners of the cells, however, did directly face each other across the hall and by quickly stepping to the corners when the guard had gone by we were able to communicate with each other.

It was an extremely slow zig-zag process, which helped pass the time of day, and accomplished what we wanted it to do. We knew that we would be tried, one at a time, and we wanted all to tell the same story. We were gong to say that the laughing that the Japanese officer heard was not for scorn or ridicule, but an expression of relief. They probably would not buy it, but that is what we were going to stick to. As it turned out this was all in vain because we were eventually released without a trial. It did help greatly, however, in making time go by more swiftly.

We were probably released when we were without the usual trial and sentencing because the Russians invaded Manchuria. Of this I am not positive, but it was either this or they knew that the war was about over for them. As I recall our release was shortly before we learned that an armistice between the U.S. and Japan was to be signed.

I did not go back to the factory to work, but instead to a small potato farm that prisoners worked for the Japanese. The farm was just outside the prison walls. We were now being fed potato soup because the Japanese were no longer able to get food supplies from the Chinese. I don't know if the Chinese were actually low on food or if they were refusing to sell because they knew that the Russians were about to defeat the Japanese. The Chinese had no love for the Japs.

At this point I would like to refer you to a diary that I started on Aug. 15, 1945 and continued until Sept. 2, 1945. It tells the story as it was happening, which is much better than my trying to recall events fifty years later. The diary is short, but I think worth including here.

★ 16 ★

Diary of James Joseph Bollich
P.O.W.
August 15, 1945, to September 2, 1945

(Original was written in pencil on lined paper. The writer was a prisoner of war of the Japanese in Mukden, Manchuria.)

Aug. 15, 1945

Sirens blew at approximately 9:30 o'clock. Was digging spuds on the farm. Came in immediately. T.K.K. came in a few minutes behind. Brought in good rumors on Russian advances. M.K.K. did not come in until noon. Also brought in good rumors. Morale very high, expect the war to end soon.

Aug. 16

No work at either factory today, although the farm workers went after spuds again. Cannot buy vegetables at the Chinese markets anymore. Food is very scarce. Came in from work at approximately 11:30 o'clock, and before stepping into the barracks, noticed a strange airplane flying low as if coming in for a landing. It did not land, however, but dropped a string of parachutes, some red and some white. Quite a few of the men saw them, and there was quite a bit of discussion as to what was taking place. Most of the men, as well as I, were of the opinion that it was practise for parachute troops because Jap fighter planes immediately began diving in that vicinity, apparently strafing because we could hear their guns. This was forgotten about shortly after it happened.

About four o'clock men from branch camp II came in, and about the same time, six new prisoners were brought in under guard of Jap M.P.'s. With these six new men came their equipment which contained red and white chutes.

Rumors started flying then. We immediately connected them with the strange large ship and the falling chutes. Between the seeing of our fellow prisoners and the stories connected with these five new men, I don't know which caused the most excitement. Rumors spread that these six men had come in to take over this camp, and that the war was over.

Americans working at the Japanese garage brought in news at about the same time that the war was definitely over. They said that a Nip told them that Japan had surrendered at 9:30 o'clock on the 15th of Aug. These men were willing to bet anything on this dope. Yes, optimism reigned supreme and never have I seen excitement such as this before. But such a heart rendering drop came in a little while later when word passed around that these six new men had been placed under lock and key in the guardhouse.

Yes, morale rating was now zero minus. The men began to think themselves foolish for letting their minds concoct such fantastic ideas. Good things like this just did not happen to a prisoner of war. Here are the steps that brought us back to earth from our quickly constructed castles in the sky. First step downwards: why should these six men, if redeemers they were, jump out in parachutes instead of coming in for a landing? Second step: had we not seen these men come in under the custody of Jap M.P.s and made to stand by themselves near the wall? There could be no doubt about it, they were prisoners just as we were. Third step:

How could anyone say that they had come to liberate us when none had spoken a single word to them and were they not now behind bars?

With the approach of night the men, dejected and heartbroken began to retire to small groups to discuss these recent happenings as they should be. That is, taking the available straight dope, and with a calm, clear mind try to dope out the situation as it should be. These confabs weren't long in session when a new hot flash spread through the camp. Without a doubt, these new men were in the Jap camp commandant's office and could be seen through the windows of our cloak room, and lo and behold there they were smoking cigarettes using matches and mechanical lighters, sitting in the best chairs, wearing wristwatches, drinking tea, and to top it off the Jap colonel was catering to them. There was no doubt about it now. From our observations we knew that something was up, and we knew that it was for the best.

Aug. 17

This morning we found out who these new men are. They are American volunteers who were flown over from China to take over this prison camp and to see that the Japanese did not mistreat us. Also to set up communications between here and our American forces. The story of their undertaking is very thrilling and these men deserve a word of praise and credit for their brave deed.

They jumped out of an American plane in enemy territory (it was still enemy territory because the Japanese here did not know of the armistice) and took the risk of being killed by the Japs. They landed safely, however, in an open field, about a half mile from this camp, and were met by Chinese farmers. A Chinese interpreter, who was one of the six, told these Chinese farmers that he wanted to be taken to this camp.

They had hardly set out when whom should they encounter but a couple of Japanese platoons armed with rifles and fixed bayonets. They were immediately taken prisoners and brought to M.P. headquarters in Mukden.

At M.P. headquarters they told their story and said that they wanted to be taken to Colonel Matsuda who was in charge of Hoten Prisoner of War Camp.

At first the Japs would not comply with their requests, because they did not know, nor would they believe that the war was over. However, after a while they talked the Nips into taking them to this camp for an interview with Col. Matsuda, still as prisoners though. That is when we got to see them.

Col. Matsuda's attitude toward them was the same as the other Japanese. As far as he knew, Japan was still at war, and they would be held prisoners until he could check out their story from higher officials. They took over this camp next morning.

In our eyes these men were heroes and to be looked up to as Our saviors. They told us what their mission was and said that help would come in as soon as possible. A radio was set up but no message could be sent out. We picked up China and the States, though, and got our first news broadcast in over three and a half years.

The American assembly call was blown at about 8 o'clock and we formed outside where General Parker (senior American officer) made a speech. Before he would cut us in on the real dope he told us that we must be calm and maintain a hold on ourselves. He emphatically stressed that there were to be no demonstrations. He proceeded to tell us of the armistice between America, England, the Netherlands and Japan, which brought a roaring cheer from the prisoners, but he warned us that we were still prisoners and that Japan and Russia were still at war.

This little speech brought happiness to everyone, even though we knew what he was going to say before he started. This was the news that they had been waiting to hear for three and a half years, and now it was official. We were still under Japanese guard but the administration of the camp was taken over by Americans. We really chowed like we should have now that we had the keys to the storeroom.

The fourteen men who were shot down in B29s in raids here on Dec. 7 and Dec. 21, 1944 were brought in today. They were living in a little stockade just outside of the walls here.

Sat., Aug. 18
Stayed up all night. Stretched blankets on the ground and held a regular bull session with American cigarettes and coffee to top it off.

Had a general cleanup and reorganization today. All organizations reformed and grouped together. General Parker was made camp commander and General Beebe was made chief of staff. General Beebe made a speech today and told us that from here on out we were again soldiers in the United States Army and to discard our P.O.W. numbers.

Russian pursuit planes flew over camp today.

Sun., Aug. 19

Held church services today in thanksgiving for the war's ending. More Russian planes overhead today. The men really get a thrill out of seeing friendly planes again. They are all anxious to see the American Air Force and its large bombers that they have heard so much about.

Mon., Aug. 20

Were told today that the Russians would be in camp. Saw our first B-24 today at about 4:30. The prisoners really went wild with joy. It circled over camp two or three times and dropped leaflets telling us about the war being over and for us to remain where we were until help arrived. These leaflets were late. They should have been dropped before the parachutists came in.

The Russians came in at about 7 o'clock and did they cause excitement. There was a general and five or six officers. The general called us all together and gave us a speech. An American prisoner acted as interpreter. The general said that from this day on we were free and no longer under the hand of the Japanese.

The crowd went wild with joy. Cheer after cheer rang through the air. He told us how in the last ten days they had covered one thousand kilometers of mountains, streams and wilderness. More cheering from the crowd. He told us that he was in Berlin when Germany surrendered and met officers of the U.S. 8th Army. He said that he told them that he would soon be leaving to fight Japan and that he would set us free.

Also had a ceremony of the surrender of the Japanese guards and the turning over of their sabers and arms to the American guards. It was quite an interesting and strange spectacle. What made it appear strange was that it was performed in the light of the moon. The Russian-General presented General Parker with a Japanese revolver. The ceremony was completed by the Russian general having the American guards parade the Japanese before the prisoners and off the parade ground.

Aug. 21

B-24 pilots came in late this afternoon. Said there was still very much street fighting going on in Mukden. From in camp it sounds like a young war going on outside, both night and day. These pilots said that they did not know exactly when we were going to get out of here, but they believed that we were going to fly out. Said that gasoline was the big problem. Left camp at dark after giving us a bit of news about home and conditions back there. Said that they would be back in the morning to take pictures to send back to the States.

Aug. 22

Russian general came in this morning accompanied by other high ranking Russian officials, among whom was a woman dressed in uniform. She attracted more attention than the general because she was the first white woman that some of us had seen in years. They inspected the camp and were supposed to have said that Russia would furnish our American planes with gas to fly us out.

Aug. 23

About twenty-six sick men left today on a B-24. Most of them were T.B. patients.

Aug. 24

Got to go to town today. The place isn't as shot up as badly as I figured it would be. The only places that are destroyed are the Japanese factories and places of business. We hired a Chinese-horse drawn cart (coo-de-ma) and rode all over the city. There are some very interesting things to see here, especially in the old Chinese walled city.

The district where the Japanese and Russians live is very modern. Inflation here is terrific. Here are a few commodities and their prices: apples, five yen; one bottle of beer, twenty or thirty; cigarettes, ten to fifteen yen for a pack of tens; matches, three to four yen for a box which sells for one cent in the U.S. (a yen at this time was valued as 0.75 of a gram of pure gold).

The Japanese people here are all confined to their residential districts. Their homes are all barricaded with high voltage wires and other impediments. The reason for this is to keep the Chinese out.

There are not many Russians in the city yet.

Aug. 25

Went to town again today. Saw the wreckage of a B-29 which was shot down in one of the raids here last December. Tried to break off a piece to bring as a souvenir to one of the guys that bailed out, but it was impossible. The B-29s are really put together. Also got in with a few Russians and I have never seen a rowdier bunch in all my life. An American officer with us acted as an interpreter. The Russians made us drink the Russian way, which is always bottoms up whenever a glass is lifted off the table. I thought this was bad enough but when they started shooting up the place, and patting us on the backs and calling us friends, I figured it was time to leave.

Visited a Dutch internee camp where Dutch Catholic missionaries were held. They were really glad to see us and welcomed us with open arms. Their life in the past years of internment was similar to ours except for treatment.

Met the French counselor's son here. It really did me good to see such a fine-looking kid again. The French counselor was not interned during the war.

176 ★ BATAAN DEATH MARCH

A lot of the men are making friends with the White Russian families here, and they all seem to be excellent people. Quite a few of them can speak English.

A lot of the men here have been given Japanese sabers by the Russian soldiers to take back home as souvenirs. They really make wonderful souvenirs.

More American planes in today. G.I.s are keeping us well supplied with cigarettes and other luxuries. They also brought in magazines, papers and books. Looking at these magazines made me realize how far advanced things are in this world and how far behind this leaves me. Anyway, it will be a pleasure catching up on this missed data when I get back to the good old U.S.A.

Aug. 28

B-29s came over today and dropped food and clothing by parachute. They really gave us a thrill because they were the first that we had seen since the raids last December. Some flew as low as a few hundred feet above the camp, and we were able to get a fair estimate of their size. It really was a relief to know that they were dropping food, clothing and medicine instead of bombs.

Hundreds of Chinese also gathered around camp to witness these beautifully colored chutes come floating to the ground. I don't know who were more amazed here, the Chinese or the Americans. It really made us feel good again to get all of this Stateside food and clothing again, and it made us much happier to know that America was going to all of this trouble just for us.

Aug. 29

More B-29s and more food and aid.

Aug. 30

Still more B-29s and aid. They are really keeping us well fed. Two American transports and a B-24 also came in today. Brought in a movie projector and films and also a large number of phonograph records and more phonographs. A colonel and his staff came in with the planes. They are to take over the administration of this camp.

Aug. 31

Another B-29 came over today. Only wanted to know how we were getting along. Said if we needed anything just let them know. These B-29s have been coming from Guam and Okinawa. The two transports and the B-24 left today with more of the sick.

Sept. 2

We have been having moving pictures now for the last two nights, and I have never enjoyed anything so much before in all of my life. Being in prison camp for so long almost made me forget what was going on back in America. I am just beginning to realize now what I have missed. If I would have seen a movie two years ago I am afraid I would have tried to escape at any cost. If I would have realized what I was really missing, this long time in prison camp would have been much harder to bear.

More sick left by plane today. Our new colonel also told us that we would probably be here for at least another month. What's a measly month more after being here for so long? In fact, it is good to know that we will be leaving for home in only one month's time.

I would like to expand on some of the things that I covered in my diary and add additional events and happenings that I feel I need to tell to complete my story.

Many years later I was talking to a geologist friend of mine who had just learned that I had been a prisoner of the Japanese. He wanted to know where I was held and I told him in the Philippines for a while and then Manchuria.

When he heard Manchuria, he said, "Not around Mukden by any chance?"

I replied Yes, and that is when he told me his story. He was the copilot of the B-24 that dropped the men by parachute, whose mission it was to tell the Japanese that an armistice was in the process of being signed and the war was over. We were flabbergasted. As they say, it is a small world.

When food and clothing was first dropped from American planes the pilots and crew tried to have it fall within the confines of the prison wall, and they did a superb job. Too good in fact, because it then became extremely dangerous. The crates and boxes of supplies were exceptionally heavy and many tore loose from the parachutes as soon as they opened. The loads in many instances were too much for the chutes. Once loose, these heavy crates came down like bombs with explosives. Some went completely through the roofs of our barracks and others smashed into outside walls and windows. Prisoners were ducking and dodging the missiles, and it is a miracle no one was hurt. Someone finally got word to the pilots to change their drop zone to an area outside of the compound.

There was still considerable danger even after all other drops were made in the newly designated area.

It appeared to be working at first because we stood back and out of the way as the stuff floated and tumbled to the ground. We were going to wait until all of the planes unloaded then pick everything up. It soon became obvious that this was not going to work, because the Chinese, who were at first taking this all in now began taking it all and running with it.

We could not stop them because there were too many so we had to rush out and salvage what we could, the danger from the air be damned.

No American prisoners were hit (we apparently were good at dodging danger), but one Chinese person was. He was cut and bleeding, but not seriously hurt. He was taken into camp and patched up and sent on his way with an armload of food.

In the process of picking up food, I came across a crate of canned fruit. The crate had torn loose from its parachute and when it hit the ground it sent cans scattering.

As I collected the cans I found a small tin of fruit cocktail

Food and clothing being dropped by American planes

that had split open. A lot of the juice and some of the fruit was gone, but instead of leaving it on the ground I picked it up and decided to eat it right then.

It was the first American food that I had had in years, and it tasted delicious, but as good as it was, I could not eat everything that was left in that can.

After only a few good mouthfuls I could not eat more and my stomach felt sick to the point where I thought I would lose what I had already eaten. This was a big disappointment to me because we had dreamed of the day when we could have all that we wanted to eat and now that it had come, look what happened.

Because of the limited amount of food that we could eat at first, it took some time to fatten us up again. At this point I probably weighed around 115 pounds or so.

When we finally got to see what the Japanese had on their side of the prison camp, we were astonished and mad. They had a room full of mail and packages from the States that they never delivered, plus a large quantity of Red Cross packages.

We speculated that the Japanese were living off our Red Cross packages when food became scarce—food that was meant for us.

I searched through the hundreds of letters scattered on the floor, but could not find one from home. I know I did not nearly go through all of them, but gave up looking when I found a package from home.

I remember it had a pack of Bugle tobacco and cigarette rolling papers, which I assumed was put in by my sister Jeanette. I also had a nice shaving brush and soap that I assumed came from Avit and my sister Jimmie and a bottle of multiple vitamins, which undoubtedly came from my parents. I know there were other things, but those are the only ones to come to mind now.

There was one person, who probably wished he had not found this one letter of his. It contained divorce papers that his wife had sent for his signature. I thought that was terrible of her. At least she could have waited until he got back home.

★ 17 ★

The Russian Encounter

By now, since we were all free to leave prison camp and wander, everyone was looking for a Japanese saber to take home as a souvenir from the war. It would show that, at long last, in the end we were the winners and they the vanquished.

On one particular day there were three or four of us that decided that we would go downtown and see if we could find Japanese with sabers. On the way we met this drunk Russian who wanted to tag along with us, since he was alone.

We were already told that if or when we met a Russian soldier on the outside greet him with the statement, "Ja Americansky Soldat." ("I am an American soldier.")

Well, when he heard we could speak Russian, he knew that he had met up with some drinking buddies. He offered us some whiskey from a bottle that he had, but we all refused. He was like most of the Russian soldiers that we ran into. They all carried at least one bottle of alcohol, usually in their back pocket with the neck of the bottle sticking out. They also carried an automatic weapon that resembled a machine-gun with its round ammunition clip.

They normally roamed around alone, such as this guy, and did not appear to belong to any organized group. They were even in Japanese uniforms (mostly officer's uniforms) and some even had their boots, which they were very proud of. I remember one showing us the picture of his young son. He was holding the son in his hand, like a waiter carries a tray of food, and the boy was stark naked.

Anyway, after awhile we realized that this drunken

181

Russian was holding us back so we decided to lose him when we could. We eventually came to some large high rise buildings surrounding a park or square (this is where we saw the downed American plane on display). The buildings were probably municipal or government, and all were empty.

This looked like a perfect place to lose our friend so we entered one of the buildings that had about ten or twelve stories. We spotted a stairway and started up with our Russian friend stumbling up behind. We stepped up our pace, and when we were about one or two stories ahead, ducked inside a door and let the Russian go on by. We listened until he was up aways and then started down as fast as we could. We were out of the building and half way across the park, when he appeared at a window yelling to high Heaven.

We knew what he wanted, but we kept running and upped our speed considerably when he started shooting at us. Some bullets came very close, but luckily we were not hit. We got away from him and went back to camp empty-handed as far as sabers were concerned.

Some of the men in their wanderings discovered a Japanese brewery on the outskirts of Mukden so they commandeered a Chinaman and his horse-drawn cart and loaded it up with beer, which they then took back to camp.

Once in camp it did not last long, so a detail was sent out to get more. They came back empty-handed, however, because the Russians had now discovered it also, and they would not give us any. I was puzzled because generally they were willing to share their liquor, but now they weren't. Probably it was already in the control of Russian officers, who wanted to keep it out of the hands of their men.

I still had not gotten hold of a saber, so one day I decided to go downtown to the railroad station and see if trains were bringing in Japanese soldiers. The first train that came in was a troop train loaded with Russians and their armaments, which was primarily tanks and trucks.

When the train stopped, I happened to be next to their

dining car. Pretty soon heads and bodies were sticking out of the car window motioning me to come on in, which I did. This was a mistake.

The so-called dining car was filthy. There were dirty dishes and glasses all over the place. I thought to myself, "I have seen and lived around filth, but why should they?"

Anyway, they sat me down at a table and invited me to eat. Apparently all the Russian soldiers had finished eating, and now had gathered around to watch me.

One of the soldiers picked up one of the dirty dishes and 'cleaned' it with his sleeve and what food remained on the plate he rubbed off with his hand.

He then filled the plate with a heaping serving of rice and something that looked like pieces of meat. You could tell it had all been cooked together in one pot. The pot was still on the table.

Another guy grabbed a dirty glass and filled it with what looked like tea. I knew there was no possible way that I could eat the mountain of food stacked on my plate, but I decided I would eat some of it.

I looked around for a fork or spoon and soon had a spoon handed to me after being 'cleaned' on this soldier's pants leg.

The Russians were not being funny or mean, but sincerely felt that they were being kind to an American soldier. I am not sure if they knew that I was a recently released prisoner.

Anyway, when I took my first bite of the rice dish I nearly choked. It was so bad that I didn't think I could get it down. To help it on its way I reached for my drink and took a swallow, which sent chills down my spine. It was tea as I suspected, but it was so sweet that it tasted like syrup.

I was in a fix now, and knew I had to make the best of it, so I would take a small bite, wash it down with a sip of tea and try to carry on a conversation by gestures.

I was hoping I could make them forget about feeding me by distracting them, but it did not work. They made me eat much, much more than I wanted, but luckily not all I had on my plate.

When we finally left the dining car they showed me their live goats that they carried with them for fresh meat. The dish that I had was cold rice and goat.

The Russians also showed me their tanks and trucks. They said that the trucks, as far as I understood, were American and so were parts of the tanks. They also showed me that their uniforms were made of American material. Knowing how we supplied the Russians during the war made me often think why we did not put up air bases on their soil to attack Japan proper. It appears to me that the war could have been won much sooner by doing so instead of our recapture of island by island in the South Pacific.

While we were out roaming we decided to go back to the factory and look things over. We were flabbergasted by what we found. The place was empty, completely stripped from wall to wall, not a single piece of machinery left. We learned later that this was looting by the Russians and took place all throughout Manchuria. It was also why they were so long in giving us train transportation out. They were using the trains to take their spoils of war back home to Russia.

By now there were many Russians in our camp. They had come in with Americans and were not officials, who had to be there, but drunks looking for a place that would feed and house them.

We were friendly Americans and they liked us. Our friendship eventually ended, however, when a trigger-happy Russian started shooting up the ceiling in one of our barracks. He was on a lower floor and luckily he did not kill or wound someone above. After this they were all made to leave and none were allowed back in unless on official business. They did not like it one bit, but it had to be done.

After the eating episode with the Russians at the railroad station, I was reluctant to go back there, but I still did not have a Japanese saber, and still thought the station offered the best possibilities of acquiring one. So back I went.

I picked a spot to sit where I could watch people as they got off the train. The spot was on top of a luggage cart, which was identical to the ones found in the States. It had a flat bed and large metal wheels and a tongue for pulling by hand.

Pretty soon a Russian soldier approached me and pointed to my new shoes. They were new army shoes that had been dropped to us by plane. Still sitting, I raised my leg so that he could get a better look then dropped it down again. He kept motioning to my feet so I raised my leg again to give him another look, but it was not another look he wanted, it was my new shoes.

He grabbed my leg and started to untie my shoe, but I wasn't about to let him have them even though he had his ever-present gun. I started kicking and pulling, but he unfortunately would not let go.

He just about had one off when luckily a Russian officer going by saw what was happening and ran the guy off.

I could just see myself walking back to camp barefoot because he probably would have taken my socks as well. I thanked the officer as best I could and got away from there in a hurry. From now on I was going to do my saber searching somewhere else.

My next saber outing was with a friend of mine. This time

Unpleasant encounter with Russian soldier

we thought we would not go into town, but would search the outskirts instead.

Someone had already scrounged some bicycles for the camp so we grabbed a couple and took off. I had never ridden a bicycle before and was a little unsteady at first, but managed somehow. After we were out some distance, we still did not see any Japanese so inquired from some Chinese if they knew of any Japanese soldiers in the area. We told them that we were looking for sabers. They did not know of any soldiers, but did know where sabers could be found. They directed us to a factory not too far from where we were. We walked in and found all Russians so we used our Russian greeting again. "Ja Americansky soldat."

We were utterly surprised when the Russian responded with, "Yes, I see that, and what can I do for you?"

He spoke very good English, and we had no trouble letting him know what we wanted. He admitted that he had swords, but said they had all been inventoried and could not give us any. He said their general was coming in soon to go over what they had and the numbers given him had to match what he had.

On the floor of this large building were hundreds of sabers and Japanese rifles, and the way they were piled up was proof in our minds that they had not been counted.

The Russian did say that if we came back in a week or so he might be able to get one for us. I suspect before a week was up they had all been shipped to Russia.

We left him and went to what looked like an office building which was part of this complex. Inside we found a single Japanese civilian, who spoke very good English.

We asked him if he could talk the Russians out of a couple of sabers, but he said he could not.

My friend then asked him if he had a saber and was surprised when he said yes. He went to the drawer in his office and came back with a beautiful hari-kari saber to show us. It was about a foot long and in a very lovely scabbard or holder.

My friend asked to see it more closely and the Japanese

obliged by handing it to him. I thought my friend had talked the Japanese into giving him the saber, and he would send him money later, but apparently that was not right, because my friend told me much later that he did not get the saber. This time we were close to sabers, but still did not have any.

I was determined that I would not leave Manchuria without a saber, so I went out again, this time with a different friend. Once again we decided to do our searching out of town and in the countryside.

We were several miles out as I recall, when we spotted a large column of Japanese soldiers marching in the road and headed our way. We figured surely some of those soldiers had what we wanted so we stepped out to the side of the road and waited for them. Pretty soon they were close enough for us to see that they were armed with rifles and sabers. This was our chance.

When they got up to us, we just walked into the column of Japanese and started taking sabers from those that had them. We probably had eight or ten right away, but before long we had dozens. As the Japanese marched by they apparently thought that we were disarming them of sabers, because everyone with a saber unbuckled it from his waist and threw it in our pile.

Because of the length of this column we had not noticed a Japanese officer on a horse, but he noticed us. He galloped up with his saber out, and he was mad.

My first reaction was that we were in big trouble now and would not only loose our sabers, but possibly our lives as well.

I don't know what my friend was thinking, but his reaction was definitely better than mine. He picked up a saber, pulled it from its sheath, walked up to the officer and with words said, in effect, "Buster, we won this war and if you don't shut up and get going, I'll cut your blankety-blank head off and your horse's, too."

I was stunned and thought, Oh, no, this is it, but sheep-

Challenging Japanese officer on horseback

ishly picked up a saber, too, like I was as bad and tough as my friend.

After a bit of loud grumbling the officer moved on. Although we got no more sabers from his troops, it did not matter because we had more than enough.

We finally found a Chinaman with a cart who helped us load up our loot and take it into camp. I picked out what I thought was one of the best of the lot and I assume my friend did the same. The rest we gave away. At last I had my saber.

★ 18 ★

Leaving Mukden

By now all of the sick had been taken out by American B-24s, and the rest of us had to wait for the Russians to provide transportation out. I was in no big hurry, but the day finally came. We were all loaded up in trucks and now on our way to the railroad station.

I was on the last truck out and as we pulled away, I saw the Russians come out of the front gate with the Japanese and walk on the outside of the brick wall toward the back of the camp. My impression was that they were going to line the Japanese up against a back brick wall and shoot them. As far as I know, we never did learn what happened to them.

Before long we were at the train station, a place that I knew very well by now. We boarded a train and were soon on our way. I no longer had to listen to the far-away sound of a train at night and long to be on my way home. Now I was actually on one and it is difficult for me to describe how I felt. It was not a dream, again. It was real.

The first song that was played in our camp, when we were provided with a record player and records was "Sentimental Journey." It seemed such an appropriate song at the time, and now its words were coming true. We were now all embarking on a sentimental journey home. Everytime I hear this song now it brings back memories of that time so long ago.

On the train we were escorted by Russian soldiers and fortunately these were of a higher caliber than the ones that we ran into on the streets of Mukden.

We found out that one could speak French and my friend

189

from Lafayette, who also spoke French, got with this Russian and had a lengthy conversation. I did not understand much of what was said, because my French was just a little better than my Russian.

I don't recall how long the train took, but I know I wasn't keeping track of time. Anyway, we finally arrived at a place called Port Arthur, a port city on the north end of the Yellow Sea. I thought it was a strange name for a Chinese port, but that is what it was called.

I remembered we had a Port Arthur in Texas and wondered if the people in Texas knew that there was a Port Arthur in China.

I believe we landed at night, but one thing that I recall with certainty is this: There was an American transport waiting for us at the dock, but when the ship's captain saw all of us armed with rifles and sabers, he would not let us on the ship unless we gave up our weapons. We said, "No way, Captain. These are ours, and we are not going to part with them."

He then said that he would safely store them for us, and they would be returned when we docked. Our reply was an emphatic no.

By now we were looking for a place to sack out because we were not going to board that ship without our arms. Well, after a lengthy delay the captain relented, and we were finally allowed on the ship with our sabers clanking on our sides.

★ 19 ★

Aboard Ship

Once on the ship we were given a cursory medical check, de-loused and given clean clothes, I believe, before being taken to our living quarters. Our dispute with the captain of the ship was over now, and everyone could relax in clean quarters on a very comfortable bed. This was the first real mattress that I had slept on since leaving the S.S. *Coolidge* almost four years ago. It felt great, and the food provided was also very good. Now our minds and bodies were truly at ease.

We were on our way to the island of Okinawa. The sea was very smooth the first few days out, and I spent a lot of time out on deck just watching the ship slice through the water.

At night I would move to the back of the ship to watch the phosphorescent glow of the water as the ship's screw pushed us along. I wasn't the only one doing the looking, though. Several of the sailors had the job of keeping a close lookout for floating mines, and they did spot several. When they were sighted, they were fired upon by what looked like .50 caliber machine-guns and small 20-millimeter cannons.

All were hit with some just slowly sinking and others exploding with a loud bang followed by a high column of water. It was exciting to watch.

After several days we finally reached Okinawa and slowly pulled into port at Buckner Bay. The weather had now turned cloudy and windy, which roughened the sea considerably, but now we were in the calmer waters of the bay.

I don't know if we ever dropped anchor, but I do know that within minutes after our arrival, we were leaving Buckner Bay and heading back out into a very rough sea.

We were soon told that a strong typhoon was headed our way and the safest place for us was in open water instead of the shallow bay. Before long the island of Okinawa disappeared in the distance, and night wasn't long in coming.

By now the sea was very rough, and it was tough just getting around for a non-sailor like myself. It was just as difficult trying to eat. Your dishes were trying to get away from you as the ship pitched and rolled. It even seemed worse when you went to bed and tried to sleep. You would roll on one side of the bunk and back to the other side. Roll, roll, roll. Sailors could probably sleep through this but not me.

I must have fallen asleep eventually, because about 4 o'clock in the morning I was awakened when the ship was rocked by a tremendous explosion. I could not imagine what it was because it was a lot worse by far than an exploding depth charge.

Our lights were now out and we were in complete darkness. You could hear people scurrying around in the dark, some wondering what was going on, and others apparently searching for their clothes so that they could get dressed and try to reach top side to find out what happened.

By now people were striking matches and lighting cigarette lighters to make some light to see by.

Before I got completely dressed, I could hear sailors working their way down toward us shouting, "Everybody topside immediately and prepare to abandon ship. Everybody topside, hurry, hurry, hurry."

It now became a mad scramble with the ship now pitching and rolling in an unbelievable way. It now was almost impossible to move without being banged into something. I don't know how we made it, but we all finally reached the top deck with the assistance of sailors, who now had flashlights and showed us the way out.

By now you knew that something was terribly wrong because the ship's engines were no longer running and without power; we were being tossed about like a cork on water.

I soon found out that this was not a good analogy, and I wished we were like a cork. A cork is unsinkable but we were not.

We had hit a mine, which tore a hole in the side of our ship and flooded the engine room, and, in turn, knocked out our power. There was a possibility that the ship might sink, which is why we were all ordered on top side, and given life preservers. We had to be ready to abandon ship if need be.

Even if we had abandoned ship, I doubt if many of us would have survived. It was still dark and on top of that there was no possible way to lower lifeboats with the ship lurching back and forth as it was.

Once on top deck we had to tie ourselves to something to keep from getting thrown off, at least that is what I did. I found a place where I could sit down and also tie myself down with the straps of my life preserver.

By now everyone was wet from the driving rain, and the wind howled and whistled. I thought to myself, Is our misery ever going to end?

Mine-damaged ship floundering in typhoon off Okinawa

When daylight came I sort of wished it hadn't. What I saw was enough to scare a person to death. We were adrift in a violent sea with waves fifty feet high. You had to look almost straight up to see their crests when they came rolling toward you. They were much higher than the ship, especially when the ship was in a wave trough.

I could not understand how the ship was still afloat in such a sea. The reason that we were was that these huge waves did not break at their crest, because if they had, they would have rolled right over us. If we had been in shallow water and the waves broke, I am sure we would have sunk.

Even though we were still afloat, there was still a worrisome possibility that the ship would go down. When the mine exploded and flooded the engine room, it tore loose one of the big steam boilers which then threatened to tear our ship apart. It could be heard as a loud bang each time it was thrown against the metal hull of the ship. It went from side to side as the ship pitched and rolled, metal against metal. It seemed impossible that the ship would survive, but it did.

The engine room was flooded, but the front and rear ends of the ship had been sealed off from the water and unless the ship was torn apart, we had it made.

It was sometime during the first day that the captain informed us that we were only two hundred miles out from Okinawa and not to worry.

I thought to myself, Captain, you might be able to swim two hundred miles, but I'm pretty sure I can't.

I did not realize at the time, but I suspect he had radio contact with other ships in the area with the radio powered by battery. I wish he had passed on this information at the same time. I think it would have eased our minds somewhat.

We stayed out on deck day and night, and it wasn't until the second day that sailors went down to the galley to get cold cuts and bread for making sandwiches. They also brought up drinks. With all power out there was no cooking possible. Although the sailors were allowed to go below deck for food, we were still told not to, not that anyone really had that thought in mind.

About the third day, however, when the sea had calmed down considerably we were told that we could go down for a short trip, but not to stay down very long. I went down to check on my saber, which was still there and also noticed to my horror that sailors were still trying to shut off water leaking through the bulkhead. We still were not out of the woods, as the saying goes.

On the third day we finally spotted another large transport ship, and it was coming our way. Eventually it got to us and slowed down. With a bit of maneuvering it finally got in position to shoot a line over to us, which we then tied to our bow.

Even though the water had calmed down quite a bit, the other ship could not tow us so we had to be cut loose.

We were adrift again. It may have been late this same day, or at the latest the next day, when we spotted a small ship off in the distance.

As it got closer, we could see that it was a tugboat, and I thought to myself, If that big boat could not pull us how did this little shrimp of a boat expect to do it.

I assumed that is what it came for. I was right on one thought and wrong on the other. The small tug had come to pick us up, because in very short order it had a line tied to our bow, and without hesitation took off with us trailing behind. It was pulling us about as fast as our ship traveled before it lost power. I later learned that this was a sea-going tug that was practically all engine. A very powerful engine squeezed into a very tiny hull. I was truly amazed.

I purposely left the most terrible part of this episode until last. Besides severely damaging the ship, the exploding mine was responsible for the deaths of about ten ex-prisoners and several sailors that were in the engine room. The ex-prisoners were on deck when the mine went off. The explosion slung landing ladders that were hanging on the side up and over the railing like lethal whips. The men were apparently killed instantly. These were the same ladders that we had used to board ship just a few days earlier. I felt depressed and I am sure that the other men felt the same. These men were on their way home after their terribly long and hard ordeal, but now they were dead. To get this far and still not make it was unbelievable.

The Japs finally got them after all with their floating mine. I couldn't help but think of the poor parents and families back home. They had been notified that their son, or husband, or brother was on his way home; you can imagine the joy they felt. Now they had to be notified that they had been killed on the way home.

I knew one of the dead men very well. It seems cruel to repeat now, but everyone called him One Eye. In the Philippines many of the prisoners developed an eye disease in which the lens of the eye turned white and became completely opaque, leaving the person afflicted almost completely blind.

This disease was similar to a disease that I saw as a boy on the farm. It was in the eyes of cattle. I never knew what caused it, but after a few weeks the eyes would clear up again and then look as good as ever.

This also happened to the prisoners. Most got over the ailment, but for some reason or other only one of my friend's eyes recovered, and the other stayed opaque. Hence the name One Eye. I am happy to say that I was not the one to name him. The one that did I am sure did it in jest.

★ 20 ★
Okinawa

When we got back to Buckner Bay we were unloaded onto small crafts which took us to shore. Now that we were close to water level we could better see the large hole in the side of our ship made by the exploding mine. I suspect that if we had to be hit, we were hit at the best place possible, or probably I should say it could have been worse.

If it had hit the front or rear compartments of the ship many more ex-prisoners would have died either by drowning or killed by the explosion. Again, if it had hit at the juncture of compartments and flooded two major parts of the ship then I think all would have probably been lost. The ship surely would have gone down and all of us with it. I hesitate to say that we were lucky, however.

I never did find out how many sailors were lost. We later heard that three bodies were still in the engine room when it was entered, but other bodies had been washed out to sea through the hole in the ship caused by the explosion.

Once ashore on Okinawa we were taken to Army barracks and treated royally. We were fed like kings. When the camp commander heard that we were interested in our new aircraft, he decided to give us a show. At the designated time different planes appeared with one group of three or four followed by another group and so on until the fighters appeared. They were not going to fly over in formation, but instead were going to give us a real show.

Before I go on with the show I have to give you an idea of the setting. Our camp was surrounded by small, tree-covered hills that were about 100-feet high. In other words, we were in a small depression that resembled a bowl. The fighters arrived one at a time, and their first pass was possibly a thousand feet or so in the air flying at maximum speed. Each pass got lower and lower, each fighter trailing the one ahead of it not more than one hundred feet. It sounded like a hornet's nest that had been disturbed, and the hornets were mad!

About then I began to become concerned for their safety, because they would come in rolling over the hills, swoop down and barely make it up in time to avoid hills on the other side.

I kept thinking, Stop, stop, we've seen enough. We don't want you to kill yourselves for our pleasure. But they kept coming.

Soon pilots were clipping leaves from tree tops. They stopped when one came so low that he hit the camp flagpole, bending it so that it looked like a capital "C." Sparks flew when the fighter hit it. The accident produced a sound that suggested a giant scratching his nails on a blackboard.

The belly of the plane was ripped open, and I expected it to immediately crash in flames, but it did not. The pilot landed safely, and we got to talk to him and the others a little later. We told them that they were crazy and that we would have been properly impressed without the acrobatics.

When we were on Okinawa some American soldiers, whom I assumed were with the post office or another governmental agency, told us that there was no sense in our lugging personal gear around anymore. Why not send it back to the States instead?

Most of us took up their offer and after tagging our bags with our home address, packed the things that we wanted shipped. I did not have much to send, but I did give them the shaving brush that I received in the package from home, silk from one of the parachutes that dropped food to us in Manchuria and a few other things, but that was it.

They wanted us to pack Japanese rifles, sabers, flags, etc., but I would not give up my saber. I was going to carry it all the way, and I am glad I did. The men that sent their sabers and rifles never saw them again, nor did I ever see my package. These men apparently never intended sending the stuff on as they said, but instead sold it. Japanese souvenirs of war were bringing big money, and is what they undoubtedly got for the stuff that they took from us. Instead of trying to help us they were robbing us blind.

After a few days on Okinawa, we were taken to an air strip, where we boarded B-24 planes and took off. Our seats on the plane were a little unusual, to say the least. They were located in the bomb bays of the huge bombers and made of 2 x 4s wedged in against the sides of the plane for the back part of the seat and the front or forward part hung from the bomb racks. You had to wonder who came up with this brilliant idea. I wonder if he was brave enough to have tried it out. Probably not.

These seats were on both sides of the bomb bay and I am now guessing that they held a total of about forty or fifty men. You climbed up on your seat through the bomb bay doors and when all the seats were filled the doors were closed, and you were on your way.

Before long all we could see was a very blue sea far below us, which was hidden occasionally by white, puffy clouds. Everyone had his eyes glued to the crack in the floor and at the same time being very careful not to move any more than necessary because of the rickety construction of the seats.

I don't know if this is true or not, but we did hear that some men were lost when the bomb bay doors opened, and the men were sucked out and fell to their deaths. I know for a fact that if those doors opened in flight, it would have been very difficult to keep from falling out, because there was nothing but the seat to hold on to. I just hope that it did not happen.

★ 21 ★

Manila

After quite a long flight we finally reached Manila. I don't remember where we landed, but it was probably Nichols Field, one of the first that the Japanese bombed when they hit the Philippines. From the airfield we went by bus to "tent city" where hundred of soldiers were assembled to await their turn to be sent home. This was where our paperwork had to start again from scratch.

Up to now none of the military had bothered to get names, outfit, rank, etc.; they just picked us up and moved us from place to place, but now it was different. Here they wanted our full story, name, rank, serial number, outfit, age, religion, etc. This was necessary, because all of our records overseas were lost.

One person that we know of took advantage of his lost records by advancing himself two or three grades. He got away with it because no records existed to prove otherwise, and those of us who knew certainly were not going to tell on him.

Some of us could have legitimately raised our grades. Before the war ended several of us had been recommended for promotions with these recommendations sent on to headquarters on Corregidor for approval. Unfortunately, approval never came because of the worsening situation on Bataan and Corregidor.

After the war we tried to get our squadron commander to verify the fact that we were up for promotion, but since he was not squadron commander at the time and had nothing to do with it, he would not go to bat for us.

He did sign a statement that read something like this: This person came to me and stated that he was up for promotion, but because of wartime conditions the promotion was never officially approved.

This meant nothing. He knew it, and I knew it. This is exactly what he gave to the other men. We should have promoted ourselves, anyway, because under any other circumstances they would have been approved. Recommendations for promotions always came back approved, and ours would have been also. When we returned to the States we were advanced one position in rank, which upped me to a buck sergeant, but the advancement was not retroactive. Had it been it would have helped our final check quite a bit.

I believe that I stayed in Manila for about two or three weeks before leaving. We were again quartered in a very large tent city. I found the food good, but other soldiers, who were not ex-prisoners grumbled about it.

This tent city was the staging area for troops ready to be sent back to the States, and it was very crowded. I did run into a few of my friends from my outfit who I had not seen since the surrender. Some had been sent to Japan, where they worked mostly in coal mines. Others stayed in the islands.

Except for being offered an opportunity to go back to Bataan for a tour, we were now part of the crowd. I don't know if anyone jumped at the chance to go back to Bataan, but I know that I did not. That place represented too much pain and suffering, and even though I had buried stuff with the intention of coming back, I was willing to forget about it. When I buried it I was thinking of returning within a few months, not several years later. Even if I had gone on the tour, it is very doubtful that I would have been taken way back into the jungle where my stuff was hidden.

While in Manila I wrote a letter or two home, but still could not receive a reply because I had no permanent address. I stayed in camp like everyone else because there apparently was nothing downtown.

I did get to see a USO show one night that was held in camp under some trees. It was singing and dancing and piano playing, which was good, I guess. I was never much for this kind of entertainment. The piano players were supposed to be the best in their field in the States. There were two of them and apparently they composed their own music. This is the only entertainment that I went to, but knowing the Army, I am sure there were movies set up somewhere for the troops.

★ 22 ★

Across the Pacific

O ne day I finally saw my name on a list pinned to a bulletin board as one leaving by ship for the States on such and such a date. We were told to be packed and ready to go. When the day arrived, we were put in trucks and taken to the docks of Manila. Before long we were all aboard and on our way.

After I placed my gear on my bunk, I immediately went on top side. I wanted to have a long last look at Bataan and Corregidor. We went out of Manila Bay just the way that we came in originally, which was the narrow pass between Bataan and Cor-regidor.

Bataan was already lush and green. The scars of war were no longer obvious, but that was not the case with Corregidor. Now it probably looked worse than it ever did because of the damage done by bombs and shells when it was recaptured by the Americans. Now it was a total wreck and the jungle growth of plants and trees had not had time yet to cover its scars as it had on Bataan.

Before long the last of the tropical islands disappeared in the distance, and we were now well out in the open ocean. There was nothing to do but eat, sleep and read, and this would go on for several weeks.

During the day I would mostly read and at night go out on deck and look at the stars. I could see the same stars that I watched while on my machine gun on Bataan, and they brought back memories that seemed ages ago. A lot had happened since then and most of it was not good, but that was in the past, and now I had an exciting future to look forward to.

My body tingled in the dark when I thought about what the future might bring. Sitting out on the deck with a cool breeze blowing and the ship gently rocking made me feel a little guilty for having it so good. By now we should be far from any floating Japanese mines, and I felt safe.

I did all of my reading lying down on my bunk, and I choose one very long book, which I thought would keep me busy for the entire trip. The book was *Pepys' Diary* and was over one thousand pages in length. It was the first book that I had read in years, and I enjoyed it very much.

We also had a Hollywood celebrity on board ship, who was also returning to the States. He stayed to himself, and we were told that he was a conscientious objector. His name was Lew Ayers, and I saw him in movies that he made after the war. I don't know how long he stayed overseas.

One afternoon when I was taking a nap in my bunk, I was awakened by a loud explosion that rocked the ship. The first thought that came to my mind was more mines, so I reached for my clothes and hastily got dressed and started for topside.

I had taken no more than one or two steps on my way out when there was another explosion just like the first. I was surprised that we still had lights and power, but now I quickened my pace because I did not want to get caught below deck when the lights went out. I noticed several others were moving out just as fast as I was.

Just about the time I reached the outer deck another ear-splitting explosion occurred, but now I saw what was going on. Instead of running in the middle of a mine field as I had visualized, I found out that the Navy men on the ship were having target practice with their big guns.

I was both relieved and angry at the same time because those guys scared us ex-prisoners to death, especially the ones who were on the ship that struck a mine off Okinawa. Someone complained to the captain of the ship. He promised no more scares. I don't think he knew of our mine episode.

After many more days of sailing we finally reached Hawaii. When we pulled into Pearl Harbor there were still many sunken ships to be seen. These were some of the ships that would have come to our rescue had they not been sunk by the Japanese. What happened could not be reversed, so I tried not to dwell on it. I had my whole future to look forward to and now wanted to forget the past.

★ 23 ★

San Francisco

At Pearl Harbor we did not get off the ship, but stayed in the port only long enough to get resupplied with food and water before lifting anchor again. It was more open water for another week when one day we spotted land and before long were going under the Golden Gate Bridge and into San Francisco Bay. We eventually docked at the same pier where we had taken off almost four years earlier.

I must mention that when we entered the bay there was a welcoming party for us. It consisted of a boat with a band on it plus many others that escorted us to our pier. Some of the boats were fire boats that could shoot streams of water high in the air. It was quite a sight, and it felt so good to finally be back in the good old U.S.A.

At the dock many soldiers were met by their families and you could see the joy in their faces as they tightly embraced each other. They had been to war and survived.

From the dock we were taken to a military establishment of some sort where we were debriefed, given our military awards, and sent to the hospital. The debriefing reminds me of something that took place when I was issued new army clothes in the Philippines. I remember the guy at the quartermaster's asking me what size shoes I wore. I told him I did not know so he measured my feet.

He then asked for my pants and coat size and once again I did not remember so he measured me again for these. When he asked for my hat size and I said, "Do they come in sizes? If so, give me a hint."

I thought he would flip. I had completely forgotten all of

this stuff and even when he told me what it was it still did not ring a bell. If he had told me that I wore size 40 shoes and my hat size was 15, I would have believed him because sizes had for some reason completely left my mind.

The guy did not know that I was a prisoner and probably thought to himself, This guy is a candidate for the nut ward.

We were taken to Letterman General Hospital in San Francisco where our clothes were taken away from us and then given pajamas and a robe to wear. I am not sure that this happened to all of the ex-prisoners, because it was possible that some were in good enough shape to move to other hospitals nearer their homes. I guess they thought that I still needed medical attention.

One of the first things that the doctor said when he saw me was, "You've had hepatitis." It was easy to spot, because my eyes were still very yellow. We were eventually given complete physicals and sent to bed. Even though I may have looked bad, I felt great.

We were fed four large meals a day. Between meals nurses brought around ice cream, candy, and cookies for anyone that was still hungry. They were obviously trying to fatten us up before we went home.

I don't know how long we stayed in the hospital, but I remember that they took us to a football game one sunny afternoon. It was a very large stadium and crowded with people, but I don't know who the teams playing were. I felt a little embarrassed, because we were in PJs and robe.

★ 24 ★

San Antonio

Finally one day I was put in a hospital car on a train headed for San Antonio, Texas. This train had no seats, but was equipped with beds only. These beds were not like a Pullman car bed that could be converted to seats, but were permanent fixtures. Also there was only one level of beds to a car. No double decks.

Each bed also had a big window the width of the bed, which was great for looking outside as we rolled along, but a little embarrassing when we stopped at a station because people could look in just as easily. Luckily, we made very few stops so not many people saw us in our pajamas.

Next day we arrived in San Antonio, and the train took us directly to the hospital. Our treatment there was excellent, just as it had been wherever we went.

We had as much food as we wanted, whenever we wanted it. We did not have to ask because it was offered to us constantly by nurses and orderlies. It was now a good life and we appreciated it, but all good things finally come to an end.

After more testing by doctors and machines we were eventually asked if we felt well enough to go home. If you said yes, they would let you go home for a visit, but they did not push you. They had to be convinced that you were telling the truth before they let you go. If you were still sick there was no way that they would turn you loose.

Finally the day came when I was called up for an interview with the doctor to see if I was ready to be discharged from the hospital. He wanted to know if I still had medical problems that I wanted to talk about, and I said I felt very good except for a couple of things. I told him I had had a very bad pain in the center of my chest, that started many months ago in prison camp that was still with me, and I also mentioned a dead place on my left leg just above the knee that also had not gone away. The dead place occurred when I was on the bridge detail in the Philippines.

He did not try to explain away my symptoms or offer a diagnosis, but did give me a choice. I could remain in the hospital longer or be discharged from it now with the option of going to a Veteran's Administration doctor later if my symptoms persisted. I decided I wanted to be discharged because I still had not seen my family yet.

After being discharged, I was given my clothes back and what a relief to get out of those hospital PJs and robe. We were also allowed to draw some money from our back-pay account. This was the first pay that I had in well over four years. Including the money drawn on my account, my final payment from the Army was about $1,600.

As I was discharged from the hospital, but still did not have my discharge from the military, I decided to go downtown with a few of the guys.

We were warned that we should not go to San Antonio alone because there were con artists all over the place just waiting to get hold of service men's money. These crooks knew that men just returning from overseas and those being discharged had more money than normal and that is what they were after.

People at the base were telling the truth because we had not been in town very long when two men approached us and said, "Welcome back, soldiers."

They struck up a conversation and I recall them talking about the atomic bomb, and how it had shortened the war. They said they were pleased because they had both worked on it.

We were sitting on a bridge that crossed the river in San Antonio when they approached us, but now they said it would be a lot more comfortable if we found a better place to rest and talk. They suggested a drinking place right up the street.

We saw what they were just as soon as they walked up to us, so they were not fooling anyone. They looked like dirty bums, and there was no way that those lying rascals worked on the atomic bomb, so we walked away from them. We hung around town for a while longer window shopping, then went back to the base.

★ 25 ★

Going Home

After a while I was finally given a pass to go home. With the pass came a train ticket that would take me to Lafayette, Louisiana, the station closest to my home. A friend of mine from Lafayette was on pass at the same time so we rode the train together.

Back then the trains were very crowded, not only with soldiers going home, but with civilians going somewhere as well.

Before we got to Lafayette, I talked my friend into staying overnight in Crowley so we could clean up and be rested for our trip home next day. We spent the night at the Rice Hotel.

Next morning I decided I needed a haircut, so went to a barber shop nearby. The barber started talking about the boys that had left to go to war, some of whom had been killed.

He then talked about a family that lived near Mowata that had two sons killed and another missing in action. He said that the one missing in action later turned out to be a prisoner of the Japanese.

I was shocked beyond belief and know I turned pale because I was positive he was talking about me and my brothers even though he did not give names. This news came as a complete surprise, but I had begun to suspect something before now.

In a letter or two that I sent home I inquired about Andrew and Stephen, but never got any information concerning them when I received mail in return. I thought maybe they had over looked my questions, or at worst they may have been wounded in the war. I knew that Stephen was in the service, but not Andrew. You can imagine my grief when I found out that they had been killed.

I just sat in the barber's chair until he finished my haircut, but was too stunned to say anything. I never did tell him who I was.

When I went back to the hotel I told my friend what I had heard. I know he felt terribly sorry for me.

Before long I decided to call my sister in Eunice to see if she could come and get me, and, of course, she was over-joyed to hear my voice. She said that she would be over as soon as she could get there.

Before long she arrived and some of her first words that she said were, "Pat, I'm afraid I have some bad news for you."

Pat is a nickname that my family calls me.

I knew what she was about to say, so I stopped her and said, "I already know about my brothers."

This was a sad reunion instead of one that should have been exceptionally joyful. I introduced my friend from Lafayette and asked my sister if she would be so kind as to take him home before me, which she did.

When we arrived at my friend's home his family all rushed out of the house and greeted him with hugs and kisses. It was obvious he was missed; they were over-joyed to have him back. We met all of his family and in a short while took off for Eunice.

To get to Eunice we went by way of Opelousas instead of Crowley. Before taking me out to the farm, my sister stopped at her house for a little while so that I could see her children again.

When they came out to meet me, I did not recognize a single one. They had grown so much and to me were now perfect strangers.

I remember my niece saying, "Do you know who I am?" I had to admit I did not.

I finally got to the farm. My mother met me at the front gate. She was crying, which I expected, and started to tell me about Andrew and Stephen. I told her I knew and everything would be all right, but she kept on crying.

We hugged each other for a while and finally I was able to shake hands with my father. He said one word, "Pat," and I said one, "Papa," and that was it. He never was much for talking, but I knew that he was glad to see me back.

While this was going on the rest of my brothers and sisters stood by in silence. I presumed they were my family, but I did not recognize a single one just as I did not know my sister's family in Eunice. I still visualized the members of my family as they were when I last saw them about five years previously.

They had all grown and changed so much I know that if I had passed them on a street somewhere I would not have known who they were. All of this came as a shock. I now felt like a stranger in my own boyhood home.

I finally got around to see other members of the family. I recognized those that were older than me, but not ones that were younger. I also learned that not only my immediate family had lost sons in the war, but two first cousins were killed as well, one on my mother's side and one on my father's.

While at home I did not do much but rest. I remember my back went out on me, and I had to go into Eunice to see a doctor about it. He said it was a slipped disc and taped me up, which is all that he could do. I later found out that there was a relationship between my bad back and numb left leg. A pinched nerve in my back, which apparently happened on the Gapan Bridge detail, had killed or damaged a nerve that went to my leg.

While I was at home my father said that if I wanted to stay on the farm I was more than welcome to do so. He said we could all farm it on shares, but I thanked him and said no.

I told him that I was going back to college and finish my degree. I also had a tempting offer from my neighbor, who

214 ★ BATAAN DEATH MARCH

was a farmer. He offered to buy me two rice combines if I would harvest his rice. That is all he wanted. The combines would be mine to do as much harvesting as I wanted to do after his crop was in.

Returning veterans had priority on machines such as this. I told him the same thing that I told my father. I was going back to school, and did not intend to be a farmer.

Under the G.I. Bill the government paid all college costs. Going back to school would be easy compared to what it was pre-war.

Now I would not have to work so hard for my schooling and could concentrate entirely on my studies.

There was not a great deal to do at home while on leave. I walked in the woods a lot and visited our old swimming hole at the big cypress tree. I thought of the fun that we used to have there and especially the mud fights that were so exciting. We were all grown-up now that is, the ones who were still alive. Such a change in five and one-half years.

I seldom went to town, but do recall being invited to a dinner at a local men's club honoring a friend and me. I was pleased to know that they did not expect a speech from us. I was also invited to go on a duck hunt by some of the neighbors, but I had to decline because I still was not feeling too well. I really wanted my leave to end so that I could get my discharge from the Army and start thinking about school.

My leave did finally end, and I returned to San Antonio to get my discharge. To my disappointment, while I was gone the Army decided that everyone with a Louisiana address would now be discharged in Mississippi instead of Texas. So it was back to Mississippi for me.

Once again I was given a train ticket and taken to the railroad station by truck. If anything, the station was more crowded than ever. There were no seats left on the train when I got there, but some of us talked the conductor into letting us ride in the luggage section of the car. Here there were no seats, but every now and then we would sit on someone's luggage. It made for a very long journey.

★ 26 ★
Discharged

The train finally arrived at Hattiesburg, Mississippi and trucks were waiting to take us to Camp Shelby. We arrived sometime during the night. I was taken to a tent, which was to be my living quarters while at the camp.

I saw no one around, but assumed since it was night everyone was all ready in bed. When my Army guide entered and turned on the light in the tent, I saw it was empty of people. All it contained was about six cots and the single light bulb hanging from the tent pole.

Someone had occupied the place before, however, because there were several empty beer bottles lying around the floor. Just as soon as my guide turned on the light he turned around and took off leaving me to myself, which was all right. I was ready to go to bed and glad that I was alone and did not have to talk to others.

Before going to bed, I decided I would first use the latrine, which was a permanent wooden building not far from my tent. After I entered the building I was followed a few minutes later by five other soldiers dressed in uniform. I could tell that they were drunk because their voices were loud and their speech somewhat slurred.

I tried to ignore them, but it did not work. They walked up to me and started complaining how they were being treated by the Army. They said that they were Puerto Ricans and treated like dirt. They said white American soldiers got much better treatment than they did, and they did not like it one bit.

They were now getting very belligerent in their drunken

state, and I was right in the middle of them and alone. I tried to tell them that I was in a tent just like they were and had to use the same facilities, but that did not help at all. I finally walked away from them, but they followed close behind still complaining.

I went into my tent and hoped to God that they would not come in because then they would see that I was alone and no telling what would happen.

By then I had grabbed two empty beer bottles, one in each hand, and waited, but they did not enter. Although I could still hear them outside, I finally decided to go to bed, but with my clothes and shoes still on. I also carefully placed several more empty bottles next to my bunk within easy reach should I need them.

Much later I finally fell asleep. When I woke up in the morning, I still had two bottles in my cot with me. If a person had walked in about then, he would have thought that I really went on a drinking binge the night before.

I forgot to mention that while at San Antonio all ex-prisoners had their papers stenciled with a prominent "J." The letter "J" probably signified that we were former prisoners of the Japanese. Now wherever you went to have something done in the service, you always received top priority, no more standing in lines, etc. All you had to do was show your "J"-stamped orders, and you were immediately taken care of. I am glad that the Puerto Ricans did not know about this because it would have proven to them that what they were saying was true.

The day after I arrived in Hattiesburg I was given my discharge. This was February 17, 1946. I had been in the service for five and one half years and those are years that I shall never forget.

I wasn't sure how I would make out in civilian life after my time in the army so I signed up for the Air Corps Reserves. If civilian life did not agree with me, I would have no trouble getting back in. Fortunately, I had no trouble coping with the outside.

Before being discharged ex-POW's were offered a 45-day, all-expense-paid stay at a fancy hotel in Miami. This also included one family member of your choice. Some of the men jumped at the opportunity, but I turned it down without giving it a second thought. I wanted out!

Once discharged, I ran into the immediate problem of trying to get out of Hattiesburg. We were taken to either the railroad station or bus terminal by the Army, but that's as far as it went. We were not provided with bus or train tickets because we were no longer in the service, but were on our own.

The lines at the ticket windows were unbelievably long and after a certain number of tickets were sold, the windows were closed until shortly before another bus or train departure.

This whole setup looked impossible to me and three other guys that had recently been discharged, so we hailed a cab and said, "Take us to New Orleans."

It cost us each a pocket full of money to get away from that crowd, but it was well worth it. We were finally free of the Army and ready to face a new and uncertain future, but we were anxious to give it a try. At least I was, anyway.

As we rode along in the taxi, I could not help but feel a little sad about leaving the Army. I was among strangers again and thought how nice it would have been if the survivors of my squadron had been reassembled after the war and all mustered out together.

To this day, there are some that I have never seen since our surrender on Bataan. We had our first reunion of the 27th Bomb Group in Savannah, Georgia about twenty-five years after the war's end. That was when we first found out who had died in prison camp and who had survived.

These reunions are now held yearly at Air Force bases throughout the south from Texas to Florida. At each we are treated like V.I.P.'s. Instead of V.I.P.'s, we prefer to be called survivors.

When we were discharged we were issued sugar-ration tickets. When I saw what they were I thought to myself, these are a bit late. How handy tickets like this would have been in prison camp. They would have provided us with sugar which would then have helped us get rid of hepatitis. At this stage of the game, I no longer needed sugar for my hepatitis so I gave my ration book to my parents.

I now had sugar, but I found out it was difficult to complete a civilian wardrobe with so many items in short supply. I remember my first cousin's girl friend was able to get me a white shirt from the store where she worked, and I was most grateful.

Finally I was able to put my uniform away and become a civilian again. I was now ready to go back to school and devote all of my time and energy to study.

When I was in the service I always felt so young because everyone else was older than me. Returning to college I felt just the opposite. I felt so much older than most of the students, and, of course, I was. Luckily, there were many veterans around that were about my age, and several much older, so I didn't feel too badly about my age.

One thing I never talked about while in college was my experience in the service. I would tell my new friends that I was a veteran and had served overseas, but that was it. I was still abiding by the military's request not to tell about your POW experience to any one.

I may not have had trouble keeping POW experiences to myself after my return, but one aspect of the experiences I did have trouble with and that was in my dreams at night. Almost every night when I fell asleep I found myself back in prison camp, and I would think to myself in the dream, How did this happen? I was sure I had been freed.

It was heartbreaking to find that I was still a prisoner. It was just the reverse of what I experienced in prison camp, when I always dreamed I was free. When I woke up during the war, I found that I was still a prisoner. But at least when I woke up as a civilian I found that I was free. As good as this felt, it was still very disturbing mentally because these dreams lasted for about ten years.

For the first few years I hated to go to sleep, but luckily the dreams became less frequent. Even now they are not completely gone.

The dream that keeps coming back most often is one in which I find myself across a large body of water. I know that I must walk for miles and miles to return to where I want to be.

In my mind I know I have made this long, long walk before, and I know how difficult and time-consuming it will be. In my dream I feel completely dejected because I wonder what could have happened to get me back to this place again, but in my dream I start walking.

This dream tells me that in the recesses of my mind I am still haunted by my participation and experiences during the Bataan Death March. It is something that will undoubtedly be there always, but even though I may not be able to control my dreams, I long ago learned to live my life as though none of this had ever happened.

EPILOGUE

In the first printing of this book, I inadvertently left out several things that I meant to include in the book, and the one that a great number of readers inquire about is, "What happened to the compass that you carried with you all through your years of imprisonment?" I wish I could say that it came home with me when the war ended, but that was not to be.

The first thing I did when I knew the war was over, and the Japanese could do nothing about it then, was to remove the loose board underneath my bunk and reach for my compass. I was shocked and disheartened to discover it was no longer there. After the many, many, chances I took keeping it with me as I was moved from prison camp to prison camp; plus the sweating I did in the meantime; now it was gone. Did some other prisoner see where I hid it, and stole it from me, or did the Japanese outsmart me at last?

I tend to believe that I fell for a Japanese setup. How convenient it was to find one board underneath my bunk that the builders of the prison barracks failed to nail down. The more I think about it, the more I believe that one board was intentionally left loose. The Japanese apparently knew it would be the perfect place for prisoners to hide their contraband, and to think I fell for it. I should have kept it in my ditty bag where it went undetected for so long.

What still puzzles me, however, is that if the Japanese were the ones that discovered the compass, why didn't they accuse me of being the owner? I was certain that if it had been found on me, I would have been shot. I came home with a Japanese saber as a war trophy, but I would like to have returned with my compass as well.

As I look back now, I realize how acquiring that saber was as dangerous as having the compass, and could have caused me and my friend our lives. How easily we could have been killed by the large column of Japanese soldiers when we made them turn over their sabers to us. We were far out of Mukden on a country road, and they were all still armed with rifles and under the command of a furious officer. I am surprised we were not shot and our bodies rolled over in the ditch. At the time, I did not realize that the Japanese military was so opposed to ending the war. Maybe they thought we were Russian soldiers.

In my book, I wrote how we were transported between Okinawa and Manila in the bombay compartment of B-24 planes. I also mentioned that I heard where several prisoners fell out of a plane when the bombay doors were accidentally opened by someone in the cockpit. I have since learned this to be true. It still bothers me to recall, how, even after beating the odds, and surviving three and one-half years of imprisonment, some men died on the way home.

Dropping the first Atomic Bombs is still a topic of much discussion today. Some say that Japan was already defeated, and the use of the bomb was not necessary. Others contend that by dropping the bomb, the lives of many Americans, and Japanese soldiers and civilians as well, were saved, because an invasion of the Japanese mainland was not necessary. What a lot of Americans still do not know is this.

Shortly before the war ended, the Japanese High Command sent out a directive to all prisoner-of-war camps, which stated that when the first American soldier landed on Japanese soil, all prisoners held would be executed. The order further stated that the Camp Commander had the option as to how it would be carried out. He could have the prisoners shot, poisoned, drowned, etc., but make sure that NO SINGLE PRISONER SURVIVED. Knowing the Japanese military, they would have gladly followed these orders.

I, plus many other former prisoners of the Japanese, are alive today because of the Atomic Bomb. Dr. Edward Teller, the father of the Hydrogen Bomb, was one who had second thoughts about dropping the bomb, but when he learned what the Japanese had planned for the prisoners in case of an invasion, he completely reversed his thinking, and agreed wholeheartedly that dropping the bomb was the proper thing to do.